323 DAYS

323 DAYS

A Marine Battery Commander's Firsthand
Account of the Korean War, 1951–1952

Transcription and Editorial by
John Harris

proving
press

Hardback ISBN: 978-1-63337-292-4
Paperback ISBN: 978-1-63337-221-4
E-book ISBN: 978-1-63337-296-2
LCCN: 2019908655

Book design and production by
Columbus Publishing Lab
47 N. 4th Street, Suite 204
Zanesville, OH 43701
www.columbuspublishinglab.com

Printed in the United States of America

CONTENTS

Dedicated to the veterans of the Korean War, 1950–1953

INTRODUCTION

I am the son of Albert and Mary Alice Harris. My wife is Joan Harris. I have one sister, Amy Jones, who lives with her husband, Larry, in Rio Rancho, New Mexico. I am a native Texan but retired to Ohio four years ago to be near my son, daughter-in-law, and four grandchildren. I like to say that, "I am the only guy from Texas who ever retired to Ohio!" Needless to say, it has been great for both my wife and me to be near our grandchildren and watch them grow up. It is amazing how busy we stay in retirement with all our grandchildren's activities, but I also have had a chance to start reading again. My reading preferences have tended to be mostly history and historical fiction.

Several months ago, I was at Half Price Books and I noticed a book jacket with a picture of a Pershing tank on it (I loved tanks growing up). It was titled *Spearhead* by Adam Makos. A quick review of the jacket revealed it was a historical account of the 3rd Armored

Division's push into Germany during World War II. The book was based on personal interviews with the various veterans in the book as well as extensive field research.

The jacket further revealed that Adam had written two other books, *A Higher Call* and *Devotion*. *A Higher Call* was about air combat in World War II, and *Devotion* was a story about the Korean War. I purchased *Spearhead* and immediately went home and ordered *A Higher Call* and *Devotion*. I read *Spearhead* first and then moved on to *Devotion*. My father was a veteran of the Korean War, and I hoped I would get a better understanding of what he actually encountered during the war.

Well, *Spearhead* was nothing short of fantastic! I felt like I was in the Pershing tank doing battle along with the crewmen. What a moving story! I then moved on to *Devotion*, a story of Navy Corsair pilots who supported Marine ground troops during the Korean War. Equally moving, I read through about half the book and remember one day thinking that I sure wished Adam Makos had interviewed my father before he passed away. Dad was a decorated Marine artillery officer. I knew bits and pieces of his story, but felt sure he could have contributed to Makos's book from an artillery support perspective.

And then it dawned on me. When my sister and I were settling Dad's estate, we had encountered numerous boxes of old records stored in the attic. In one of the boxes, we had found a stack of letters Dad had written to Mom from the war.

I thought I had them somewhere, so I immediately stopped what I was doing, went down to the basement, and found them. There were over fifty letters bound with a piece of string. A quick reading of four or five letters revealed both a love story and a firsthand account of the war, including pictures and graphics. I probably had more in those letters than could have been recorded in a series of personal interviews.

Right then and there, I made a commitment to transcribe all the letters in chronological order to document my father's service during the war. I would include my own recollections, as well as those of my family, and research and document facts and events uncovered during the transcription.

I finished reading *Devotion* (which was truly outstanding) and have put *A Higher Call* on hold while I immerse myself in this project. I look forward to giving it as a present to my family, including Dad's grandchildren and great-grandchildren.

As I compile this project, it amazes me to think of all the events that transpired to make this happen. From Dad having written the letters sixty-seven years ago, to Mom having saved them through numerous moves around the country. My sister and I easily could have missed them when settling the estate, and by pure chance I found and read the books by Adam Makos, which led me to rediscover the letters. Pretty incredible!

One final note. The transcription of the letters is basically verbatim, with only minor punctuation changes. I have also edited out most personal exchanges from Dad to Mom. The war story, however, is complete, and after much consideration, I decided to leave the derogatory language intact. It is a part of the Korean War history.

Dad would have been amazed to know that sixty-seven years after writing the letters, the two-year-old son he wrote to and missed so much would be transcribing and telling his story for generations to come.

I am honored to do it.

John Harris
Maineville, Ohio
May 4, 2019

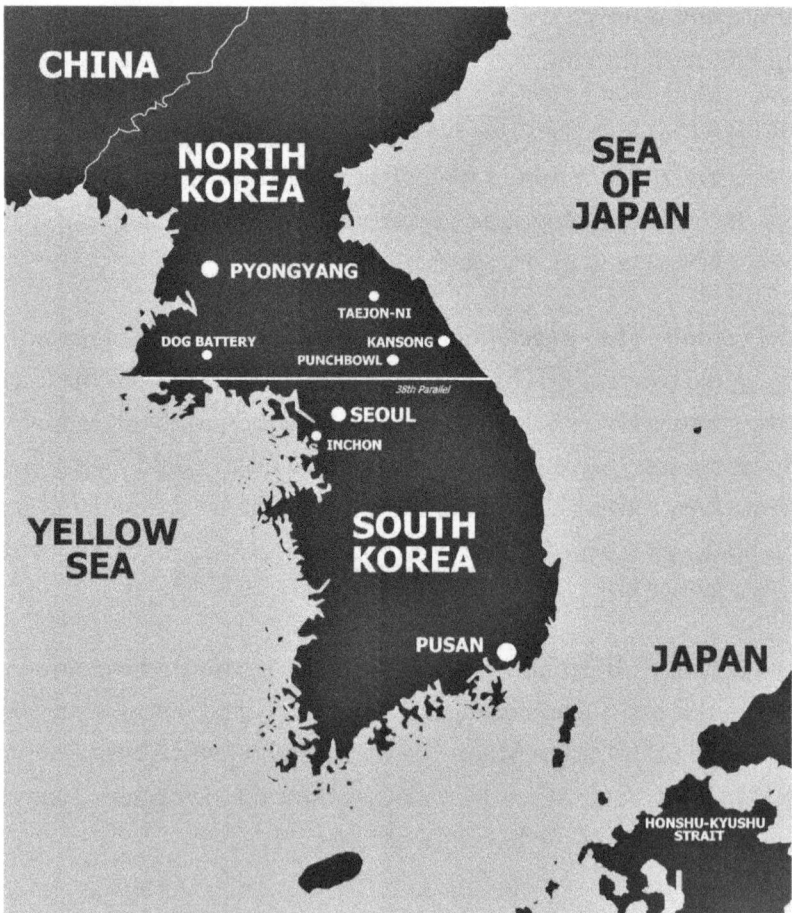

Chapter 1

PRE-WAR HISTORY

Albert G. Harris (Al) and Mary Alice Norwood were junior high school sweethearts in Greenville, Texas. As far as I know, neither ever had another girl- or boyfriend.

Mary Alice was one of four Norwood children, all of whom were very accomplished. Her father was a district attorney and subsequently elected county judge in Greenville.

Al was also very accomplished. He had one younger brother, and his parents owned a retail clothing store in downtown Greenville. Al was quarterback and captain of his high school football team, a good student (excellent in math), a skilled artist, and a leader. He had a dog named Beans that he would send to Judge Norwood's house to summon Mary Alice when they were dating in high school.

Al and Mary Alice both enrolled at East Texas State Teachers College (ETSTC) after graduation from high school, and Al joined the Marine Corps at the end of his freshman year, in 1943. Al served during World War II, but never saw active duty.

Christmas card to Mary Alice, 1944

In August of 1945, Al was commissioned as 2nd lieutenant and was shortly thereafter stationed at Camp Pendleton, California. At some point in that time frame, Al proposed marriage to Mary Alice. Mary Alice accepted his proposal and decided to take a bus to Camp Pendleton and get married.

Judge Norwood was *not happy* about his daughter traveling to California to get married. I don't think his objection had anything to do with Al, because he had known him for many years. I think Judge Norwood simply wanted Mary Alice to have a proper wedding at a church in Greenville. But that was not to be.

On February 21, 1946, the *Greenville Banner* ran the following story:

Miss Mary Alice Norwood Weds
Lieutenant Albert G. Harris
at Ceremony Held in California

Judge and Mrs. H.O. Norwood, 2212 Sayle St., announce the marriage of their daughter, Mary Alice, to Lieutenant Albert G. Harris, son of Mr. and Mrs. A. G. Harris, 3415 Henry St.

The beautiful and impressive double ring ceremony was celebrated Saturday, February 16th, at 6 o'clock in the evening in the home of Chaplin John H. Craven, Camp Pendleton, Oceanside, California. Chaplin Craven officiated at the service.

The bride wore a two-piece gray wool suit, made bolero style with sleeves gathered at the wrist. Her accessories were in black and she wore a corsage fashioned of gardenias.

The couple was attended by Lieutenant and Mrs. K. E. Davis.

Mrs. Harris graduated from Greenville High School in the class of 1942, was a member of the Sigma Tau Delta

English fraternity and the National Honor Society, and was president of the Junior Standard Club. She holds a degree from East Texas State Teachers College in Commerce, where she was an honor graduate in the class of 1945. She was listed two years in Who's Who, and served as president of the Tooanoowe Society club, president of the Alpha Chi honor fraternity, president of the dormitory counsel, and club counsel foreman. Prior to her marriage, she held a teaching position in Mertzon public schools.

The groom, who is now stationed at Camp Pendleton, Oceanside, California as an artillery officer, is a graduate of Greenville High School in the class of 1942, and was also listed in Who's Who. He was attending East Texas State Teachers College at the time of his enlistment in the Marine Corps in July 1943, and was a member of the Artema Club, a member of the library staff, and art editor for the East Texas State yearbook.

Lieutenant Harris received sixteen months of training at Louisiana Polytechnic Institute in Ruston, Louisiana, took boot training at Paris Island, South Carolina, pre-OCS at Camp Lejeune, North Carolina, Officers Candidate School at Quantico, Virginia, and was commissioned August 1, 1945, in the upper 10% of his class.

Lieutenant and Mrs. Harris will be at home in Oceanside, California for the present.

Mrs. K. E. Davis, Sr., of Houston was a guest at the wedding.

And so it was that Mary Alice (Mom) and Al (Dad) got married. One of the funny family stories that has been told more than once occurred at Camp Pendleton shortly after they were married.

They were living in a Quonset hut on base at Camp Pendleton. There is no doubt that Mom had made it clean, neat, and decorated as best she could with what possessions they had. Proud of his new wife, Dad invited several of his officer friends over for dinner one evening.

Mom outside the Quonset hut

Knowing Mom, she had the table set beautifully, and I can see her dressed perfectly, wearing a crisply ironed apron. She was preparing a fried chicken dinner for everyone.

With everyone seated at the table, it was time to eat. Mom brought out the main course—a beautiful plate of fried chicken. Every piece was evenly browned on all sides. It looked delicious, but when the first bites were taken, the chicken was raw on the inside! Mom had never cooked fried chicken before and did not realize it needed to remain in the pan for fifteen or twenty minutes to make sure the pieces were thoroughly cooked. It's funny now, but I'll bet Mom was sure embarrassed at the time!

Harris Second In U.S. With Display

Albert Harris III, display director for Garner-Avis Co., has been informed by telegram that his recent window of Flexees foundation garments for "The Dependable Store" has won second prize for the United States in its division.

The award brings a substantial government bond for Mr. Harris and a Bulova wrist watch for Mrs. Esther Malone, head of the ready-to-wear department at Garner-Alvis Co.

Winning prizes is growing into a habit with Mr. Harris, who recently won third place in the nation for this size store with his display of nationally distributed "Resistol" hats for men.

Approximately six months later, at the Naval Air Station in Corpus Christi, Texas, Dad received a certificate of honorable and satisfactory service in World War II and was discharged from the Marine Corps. A month prior to his discharge, he had applied for and received a permanent appointment to officer rank in the Marine Corps Reserve.

I am not exactly sure of the sequence of events, but I believe Mom and Dad then moved back to Greenville, where Dad re-enrolled at East Texas State Teachers College, probably in the fall semester of 1947. How he and Mom got to Brownwood, Texas, I do not know. But in 1948, Dad served a stint as display director for Garner-Avis Company in Brownwood, where he received awards for his work.

Award-winning Resistol hat display

On August 1, 1948, Dad was appointed to the rank of 1st lieutenant in the Marine Corps Reserve.

I was born July 29, 1949, the same year Dad graduated from ETSTC with a bachelor's degree in mathematics. Dad went on to earn his master's degree in education from Louisiana Polytechnic Institute in 1950.

Dad, Mom, and me (age 1 month)

Chapter 2
THE KOREAN WAR

Since the beginning of the 20th century, Korea had been a part of the Japanese empire. After World War II, it fell to the Americans and the Soviets to decide what should be done with their enemy's imperial possessions. In August 1945, two young aides at the U.S. State Department divided the Korean peninsula in half along the 38th parallel. The Russians occupied the area north of the line and the U.S. occupied the area to its south.[1]

Five years later, the communist leader of North Korea, Kim Il Sung, decided to attempt to reunify Korea under his control [with the approval of Russia]. In June of 1950, 75,000 soldiers from the North Korean People's Army (NKPA) poured across the 38th parallel and invaded South Korea. The NKPA, armed with Soviet tanks, quickly overran South Korea, and the U.S. came to South Korea's aid. General Douglas MacArthur, who had been overseeing the post-WWII occupation of Japan, commanded the U.S. forces, which now began to hold off the NKPA at Pusan, the southernmost tip of Korea. As far as the U.S. was concerned, this was a war against international communism. "If we let Korea down," President Harry Truman said, "the Soviet[s] will keep right on going and swallow up one [place] after another."[2]

At first, the war was a defensive one—a war to get the communists out of South Korea—and it went badly for the Allies. The North Korean army was well-disciplined, well-trained, and well-equipped. [Soldiers in the] South Korean army, by contrast, were frightened, confused, and seemed inclined to flee the battlefield at any provocation. Also, it was one of the hottest and driest summers on record, and desperately thirsty American soldiers were often forced to drink water from rice paddies that had been fertilized with human waste. As a result, dangerous intestinal diseases and other illnesses were a constant threat.[2]

By the end of the summer, President Truman and General Douglas MacArthur had decided on a new set of war goals. Now, for the Allies, the Korean War was an offensive one: it was a war to "liberate" the North from the communists.[2]

On September 15, 1950, a U.S. Marines force made a surprise amphibious landing at the strategic port of Inchon, on the west coast of Korea. The location had been criticized as too risky, but MacArthur insisted on carrying out the bold landing. Afterward, the American-led UN (United Nations) force was able to break North Korean supply lines and push inland to recapture Seoul, the South Korean capital, thus changing the course of the war.[3]

Marine landing at Inchon

But as American troops crossed the 38th parallel and headed north toward the Yalu River, the border between North Korea and Communist China, the Chinese started to worry about protecting themselves from what they called "armed aggression against Chinese territory." China sent troops to North Korea and warned the U.S. to keep away from the Yalu boundary unless it wanted full-scale war.[2]

As President Truman looked for a way to prevent war with the Chinese, MacArthur did all he could to provoke it. Finally, in March 1951, MacArthur wrote in a letter, "there is no substitute for victory" against international communism. For Truman, this was the last straw and the president fired the general for insubordination.[2]

General Matthew Ridgway took over MacArthur's command and held off the communists with strong fortifications and entrenchments just north of the 38th parallel. Troop morale improved dramatically. The U.S. tried using strategic bombing to intimidate the communists into negotiating a peace treaty, but the communists wouldn't budge, particularly on the issue of POW (Prisoner of War) repatriation. Neither side wanted to appear weak, and so the talks went on through 1951-1952, occasionally breaking down for months at a time.[3] The fighting during this time period was intense and both sides were entrenched, many times only a few miles apart. It was during this period that Lieutenant Harris served in the war.

Finally, in July of 1953, the war came to an end. Nearly five million people had died, including 37,000 Americans killed in action (KIA) and 100,000 wounded in action (WIA). The armistice agreement allowed the POWs to stay where they liked, drew a new boundary near the 38th parallel that gave South Korea an extra 1,500 square miles of territory, and created a 2-mile-wide "demilitarized zone" that still exists today.[2]

Korea has been called the "forgotten war" since at least October 1951 when *U.S. News & World Report* gave it that name. In reality, though, Americans did not so much forget the Korean War as never think about it at all. When the war first broke out, people worried that American involvement would usher in the same type of rationing and full mobilization [industry producing massive amounts of war goods] that had characterized WWII. Those things failed to occur and within a few months most Americans turned back to their own lives, ignoring the conflict raging half a world away. Newspapers continued to report on the war, but with the entrance of the Chinese [into the war] in late fall 1950 and the resulting stalemate in late 1951, few Americans wanted to read or think about Korea.[4] But make no mistake, it was not forgotten by the soldiers and their families. The Korean War was as brutal as it gets.

Chapter 3

VOYAGE TO WAR

As Dad was graduating with his master's degree, and I was one year old, the Korean War erupted amidst a frightening Cold War backdrop. Dad was an artillery officer in the Marine Corps Reserve, and the military replacement drafts were starting. He knew his number was coming up soon.

Dad reported for active duty on March 18, 1951. Mom and I accompanied him to Camp Pendleton, California, where he resumed his position as 1ˢᵗ lieutenant and prepared to leave for the Korean War. I believe we were housed in a Quonset hut similar to the one Dad and Mom stayed in when they were first married. In early June, my mother's twin brother, James (Offie) Norwood, drove to California to move Mom and me back to Greenville. Dad boarded ship on June 17, 1951; his letters started the next day and continued for 323 days.

LETTERS ADDRESSED FROM:

1ST LIEUTENANT A. G. HARRIS

D COMPANY, 10TH REPLACEMENT DRAFT

CAMP JOSEPH HEADQUARTERS PENDLETON

OCEANSIDE, CALIFORNIA

MONDAY 8:45 AM
18 JUNE 1951

Dear Mary Alice and John,

I'm aboard ship and still sitting here in San Diego Harbor. I got aboard yesterday about 10:30 and was assigned to a state room with 12 other officers. The room is a bit crowded, however everything is as nice as can be. The bunks are along the bulkhead (wall) three high. I sleep on the top one. We each have a wall locker in which the space is very limited. In this I have placed part of my pack, shave gear, etc. I am furnished with linens and towels so I won't have to dirty mine until I get where I'm going. Since I am a first-class passenger here, my accommodations are top rate. We will have fresh water showers all the way across and of course there will be no water ration provided everything goes OK. We eat at the officer's mess that is as nice as the Adolphus dining room—table cloths, a steward (waiter) for each table, silverware strung out on both sides and menus. The food is as good as I have eaten in this outfit. In fact, I'm doing very well and I believe it will be a pleasant voyage.

We have about 4,200 men aboard. Here are some facts about the ship's history and characteristics. The General William Weigel was built by the Federal Shipbuilding Corporation at Carney Island, New Jersey in 1943. During World War II, the ship was operated by the Army Transport Service. For several years after World War II, it operated as a troop transport carrying troops and dependents before being de-activated and assigned to the mothball fleet. Upon reactivation during the month of August 1950, the ship came under the operation of the Military Sea Transportation Service. Statistics of interest are as follows: length 622 feet, breadth 75 feet, draft 28 feet, gross tonnage

19,000 tons, crew 297. Some of the boys who have been over before say this is the biggest ship they have ever sailed on. Jones says he thinks this will be like riding on a train. Ha Ha! I sure hope it is. Of course, we don't know what port we will land in, but this is the word that is continuously drifting down the line. If we go to Japan, we will go the short route. That is, we will go along the coast of California up to Alaska and down to Japan. You might get a globe and look this up. We will sail today at 1400 and before we hit the open sea, we will have our first abandon ship drill. After that, we will have them every three days.

Honey, yesterday when we left Oceanside, I saw you and John down there on land. You were looking for me but we went by just a little too fast. I am going out on the ship in just a few minutes to see if I can see you which I doubt very seriously. I hope I can. Gosh there are so many people it will be hard to pick you out. Baby, I expect I better get down and take a seasick pill and get this in the mail before they pull the last mail off. I want this to be at home waiting for you. If I have time, I also want to drop Mother and Dad a note before we sail. I sure hope you don't have any trouble getting things packed up to move home. I would sure like to see Offie today but I guess that will not be possible. By the way, my wife and little John sure gave me the right thing on Father's Day. I'm going to have a lot of fun lolling around in them.

Honey, I'll go top side now and see if I can see you.

I love you as ever,

Albert XX [kisses]

P.S. I just got a call that last mail is going ashore.

∝✕✕○

In June 1940, the Navy had 4,007 African American per-sonnel. All the African Americans were enlisted men and, with the exception of six regular-rated seamen, all were steward's mates. They were characterized by the black press as "seagoing bellhops."[5]

Dad's report of a steward (waiter) for each table corresponds exactly with Adam Makos's account on the aircraft carrier Leyte during the Korean War: "Black stewards slipped be-hind the seatbacks and lowered silver trays of food in front of the officers. The stewards wore clean, high collared jackets and their hair was neat and closely cropped."[6] There is little doubt the stewards on board the USS (United States Ship) **General William Weigel,** *serving Dad and his fellow of-ficers, were African American enlisted men.*

At the time of the Korean War, some progress had been made in the underutilization of African Americans, but make no mistake, racial prejudice was a part of daily life in the armed forces in the early 1950s. I particularly like Adam Makos's attention to the role of the African American soldier and the difficult issues he faced in both **Spearhead** *and* **Devotion.**

Dad mentions that the officer's mess was as nice as the Adolphus dining room. The Adolphus was the premier hotel in downtown Dallas, Texas, and dining there was as nice as Dallas had to offer in the 1950s.

On the Leyte aircraft carrier, steaming towards Korea, a war correspondent recorded a typical (officers') meal: "Bean soup with crackers, grilled beef steak, mashed potatoes, mushroom gravy, creamed peas and carrots, buttered cabbage, lettuce and tomato salad, peach pie, bread, butter and orangeade."⁷ This was definitely Dad's style of food.

∝≫×⊂

SUNDAY 24 JUNE 1951

Dear Mary Alice,

It was just a week ago that I came aboard the USS William Weigel. I can say that I've spent many more enjoyable weeks than the one that has just gone by. This life aboard ship as a passenger is very tiring. Perhaps if one had any duties in navigating, or it really doesn't matter, just some specific job, the life aboard ship would be a great deal improved. That is for me anyway. All there is to do is eat, sleep, read, walk around, play cards, write, look at nothing but water, go to a show every night or play bingo. Now you might say that sounds like a life of leisure, and I guess it is, but I still don't go for it. I like the wide-open spaces (DRY WIDE-OPEN SPACES). Now that I've started on space, I might as well continue and say that I've seen absolutely nothing in this ocean but water since we left San Diego. About the second day out, some of the boys said they saw a whale early that morning, however I was in my rack (bed) and missed that. It sure gives a person a strange feeling to be so far from nowhere. I've wondered about sailors of olden days and how they fared for months at a time. We have so much more today than they in their wildest dreams conceived.

When we left San Diego, we went straight out from the coast for about 50 miles and then turned north-north-west and went straight up the coast. Off the state of Washington, the course was changed to approximately west-north-west until we reached the 49th parallel where we are sailing along this line, and sometime tonight, we will cross the 180th meridian. At this point, because we are running away from the sun, we will lose 24 hours. This means there will be no Monday. To lose a day just like that is something new to me, however I won't feel too bad about it because on the way back I'll regain a day.

The weather on the trip so far has been very smooth except for the second day. That day the boat rolled, rocked, and pitched. There were many people that were seasick. The small box of pills you bought me must've done the trick because I have yet to be sick. I've taken only five and that was during the first three days. Since then, I guess you might say I've got my sea legs because it just doesn't bother me. Of course, the ship doesn't bounce around like the little fishing boat we were on, but it does have a very definite roll. A good thing that I see about these modern-day ships is the light fixtures, etc. are all secured to the bulkhead and ceiling. There is no swing whatever. It's a good thing too, because that would sure give it to you if anything would. Poor Jones got seasick as soon as we were out of San Diego Harbor. He stayed in the sack for four days straight and here lately gets up only for short periods of time.

This is a very fast ship—goes about 20 to 23 knots and we expect to make the trip in 12 days. We have a movie every night at 1900. They are generally B pictures with a few westerns thrown in. You know, Johnny McBrown, Rocky Lane, etc. We get a kick out of them though. Twice a week we play bingo. We buy cards, three for a dollar, and play for many prizes. The prizes include clocks, watches, pen and pencil sets, luggage, etc. They also give away cash prizes. The first night $86 was given away while the last time $107 was given away. Out of the $107, $90 was given away at one whack. I came very close to taking that one, but my number just didn't come up. We will only have one more game and this one will be a big one. Hope I can do some good, but haven't yet so far. Baby, I'll write some more tomorrow. Love and sweet dreams.

MA [Mary Alice] X
John X

⁓✕✕⁓

Dad loved western movies and I imagine he was pretty rowdy when the B-rated westerns were shown. After we moved to Houston, Texas, in 1957, Dad and I never missed a TV episode of **Gunsmoke** *or* **Have Gun Will Travel.** *Those were serious westerns to us. Westerns, for the most part, faded from the big screen, but in 1985, Dad was thrilled to read Larry McMurtry's award-winning novel* **Lonesome Dove.**

⁓✕✕⁓

TUESDAY 26 JUNE 1951

Dear Mary Alice and John,

Well, it was a long night's sleep last night, or so it might seem, because this morning is Tuesday and last night was Sunday. As I explained, we lose a day at the 180th meridian. As it now stands, we only have approximately 4 more days at sea. We plan to pull into Japan sometime Saturday. The port of call is not yet known but as soon as the word is passed, I'll let you know. The weather today is very rough, in fact we have been bucking about a 45 to 50 mile an hour wind all day. The swells in the ocean are pretty good ones too.

Memento given aboard the USS *William Weigel*

THURSDAY 28 JUNE '51

Well, I'll start again today and try to bring you up-to-date as to what has been going on. One of the most interesting things that has happened are the bingo games. Last Tuesday night, John Adamson won $105 plus a billfold to carry the money in. Last night (Wed) I won $10 the very first game played. This is not much but it does bring me back to two more dollars than I had when I came aboard ship. We play 10 games of bingo at one setting, each person having three cards that are purchased for $1.00. In case there is a tie in the game, the winner is decided by a cut of the cards. I won the 10 spot on a cut.

This morning I went out on deck for a breath of fresh air about six and I was very surprised to see the ocean crawling with sharks. We are surely getting close to land of some sort, because we also see large swarms of birds. I guess in the next day or two we will begin to see Japanese fishing boats. Last night was the roughest part of the voyage. The bow of the ship was actually going underwater and the screw was coming out of the stern. The chains were rattling and the seams were creaking. For a time there, I was wondering whether this thing was going to hold together (funny thing I didn't get seasick). Jones went back to his rack and is still there.

Each day, a paper is put out aboard ship. I've been saving my copies and I will forward them on to you as soon as I can buy more stamps. I also went to church last Sunday and enjoyed the service very much. We have a Catholic chaplain who conducted the service. You see, on Sunday there are services for every faith and they are each conducted at different times but by the same chaplain. He is as nice a man as I have ever known and he certainly knows a lot about the church world. Read some of his columns in the papers.

Honey, I'm going to stop this now and write Dad and Mother. I haven't written them yet. So, bye for now! See you tomorrow.

⚬✕✕⚬

I feel sorry for Jones. If you have ever been seasick, you know what I mean—it is pure misery. Later in life, Dad

and I fished numerous times offshore in the Gulf of Mexico.
I always had to take a Dramamine pill, but Dad never did.
He maintained his sea legs for the rest of his life.

∞✕∞

29-FRIDAY-JUNE 1951

Baby, this is our last day aboard ship, because tomorrow we will dock in Japan. Now it is not certain yet as to the port of call, however the word has been passed that we will go into Yokohama to let the Army personnel off. It is known that there is an Army base located there. Now I'll have to finish this letter up tonight because tomorrow morning will be the last chance we will have to place mail in the bag here aboard ship. I want to get it in the mail then so it will be picked up by a mail boat that will meet us in the harbor. As soon as I get ashore and have a chance, you can bet more word will be on the way.

Today we have seen one large tanker and many small fishing boats of the ocean-going type. What I mean here is that they will go out at least 500 miles. The fishing craft are from Japan. The weather today has been fine but rather hot. Had to go down in the hole and check [the men's] 782 gear. Boy I was ringing wet when I came out. Adamson and I took a few pictures this afternoon and we are going to try and have them developed in Japan. If this can't be done, he will send them to his wife in California and have them done there. Nevertheless, someway, somehow, I'll see if I can't get you some prints. I also went to the ship store and bought a roll of 135 mm color film. I'll try and take pictures as we go into Tokyo Bay. This is Yokohama. The boys that have been there say it is very beautiful with the mountain (FUJIYAMA) in the background. Tonight, we had the captain's dinner. This is the feed that the captain puts on just before we leave the ship. I'll have to stop now to play bingo. Let you know how I come out …

Well, I finished last in bingo and didn't win a thing. They gave many good prizes away—camera and around $200 in cash—$110 in one whack. Also, other prizes. A fellow, Jim Mills from Dallas, who sacks across from me, won $55 of the $110. He and another guy tied.

Now, getting back to the captain's dinner, it was sure good and the dining room was set beautifully. I will be sending you a menu that was used and you can see what we had.

Honey, I had better end this now so I can get it in the mail tomorrow morning. But before I go, for now I want you to know that I was certainly glad to see you and John come walking down the dock just before we pulled out. I had seen you earlier Sunday morning in Oceanside. You didn't see me, not because you weren't trying though, but because you were looking each bus over good. I was on the third bus and we were going fast. You are a mighty swell wife, honey, and I was as proud of you as I ever will be when we pulled out. You are a good little Marine. Always remember I love you and no matter what comes, I always will. Hold tight, sweetheart.

Your husband,
Albert

MA X
John X

GOOD NIGHT (10 PM FRIDAY) 29 JUNE 51

∞✕∞

782 gear—also called "deuce" gear—included a pack, canteen, poncho, ammo pouch, etc., and was used when in the field. 782 refers to the Department of Defense (DoD) form signed when the gear was issued.[8]

∞✕∞

1:40 PM 30 JUNE 1951

Honey, we will soon be in. About another three hours. The weather is dark and cloudy with some rain. The war news sure sounds good. What do you think about the 4 divisions of Marines provided the President signs the bill?

Sugar, *I love you* and will write again soon.

Al

∞✕∞

For the most part, Dad remained positive about the peace talks throughout his tour of duty. The prospect for peace always seemed right around the corner, but would not come for another two years.

2 JULY 51

Dear Mary Alice,

We are docked here in YOSHIKAWA. This was one of the largest naval bases the Japanese had during the war. It is just about 1 ½ hours by train from Tokyo. Liberty is expected any minute now, and I'll go there for the day. Jones, Adamson and I will see the place together. Yesterday afternoon we went to shore in YOSHIKAWA. The town is large and I would say it is typical oriental. The houses, men and women, and transportation all look like pictures I have seen of the Orient. The people and their economy are about 1850 I would say. Saw many beautiful things to buy in town, however I haven't purchased anything yet. I will look around Tokyo first. I was paid $50 yesterday in a Military Payment Certificate [MPC]. The use of U.S. money is prohibited. We exchange these certificates at the rate of 360 yen to the dollar. I saw some beautiful paintings done on silk for 250 yen each. I expect I will buy some today and send them to you.

Dad (left) in YOSHIKAWA

We will leave here tomorrow morning early and go back to YOKOHAMA to pick up more Army personnel. Expect to be there approximately two days. From there, we will board ship and go to PUSAN. No assignments have been made as yet but the orders are aboard and we will get them on the way to PUSAN. I will write you then, and maybe I can give you my address. I have been feeling fine. The war news sure sounds good, but think we will get there before anything is settled. Sure would like to see them end this thing up. Baby, this is a short letter, but next time I'll try and write more. Take care of our boy and know I love you.

Love,
Al

P.S. The children here in Japan are as cute as they can be. I guess that children all over the world are much alike because the ones I've seen act much like our John does. Women here carry them on their back.

Be sweet.

XX

∞⟨⟩∞

Yoshikawa and Yokohama are both smaller cities located inside the greater Tokyo metropolitan area. The USS **William Weigel** *had essentially sailed into Tokyo Bay to dock, take on more supplies, and pick up more soldiers. It would then sail south down the eastern coast of Japan and through the Honshu–Kyushu Strait to Korea.*

Right off the bat, you see the artist in Dad. He gets off the boat in Yoshikawa, and his attention is drawn to the Japanese artists and their beautiful silk paintings. I'm sure their work was very nice and they were a genuine bargain at 69 cents each, even in 1951 dollars. Dad's creative and artistic abilities would go on to play a small but important role in his tour of duty.

JULY 7, 1951

Dear Mary Alice,

Baby, you will have to excuse the condition of this paper because I've had it in my pack for the last two days. I will try to bring you up-to-date now. We left YOKOHAMA on July 4 for PUSAN and arrived here early the morning of the 6th. The trip over was beautiful and especially so when we went through the straights between the main island of Japan HONSHU and a smaller one KYUSHU. Saw many quaint oriental pieces of architecture along with quite a few oriental customs. Looked as though I was in a storybook world. Then we landed in PUSAN.

I will have to wait and tell you some of the things that I saw on the way in. It's absolutely unbelievable in this day and time. I am now in an army transit center approximately 5 miles from the heart of the city. I will be here until Monday or Tuesday, at which time I will take a plane load (38 men) up to the 11th Marine Regiment. The trip will be in three phases. (1) We leave here by truck and go 20 miles over high mountains to the airport. After reaching the airport (2) we will fly about 120 miles north to another airport. (3) There we will change planes and pick up a fighter escort to within approximately 10 miles of the front. This is where I'll join up with the regiment and be further assigned to a battalion and then to a firing battery. As soon as I get down to the lowest echelon that I'm going, I'll send you my address and my mail will come much faster. I got my first letter from you on the 3rd of July in YOKOHAMA. It was so good to hear from you and know that you got home safely. I know Offie had a hard time going all the way to California and then

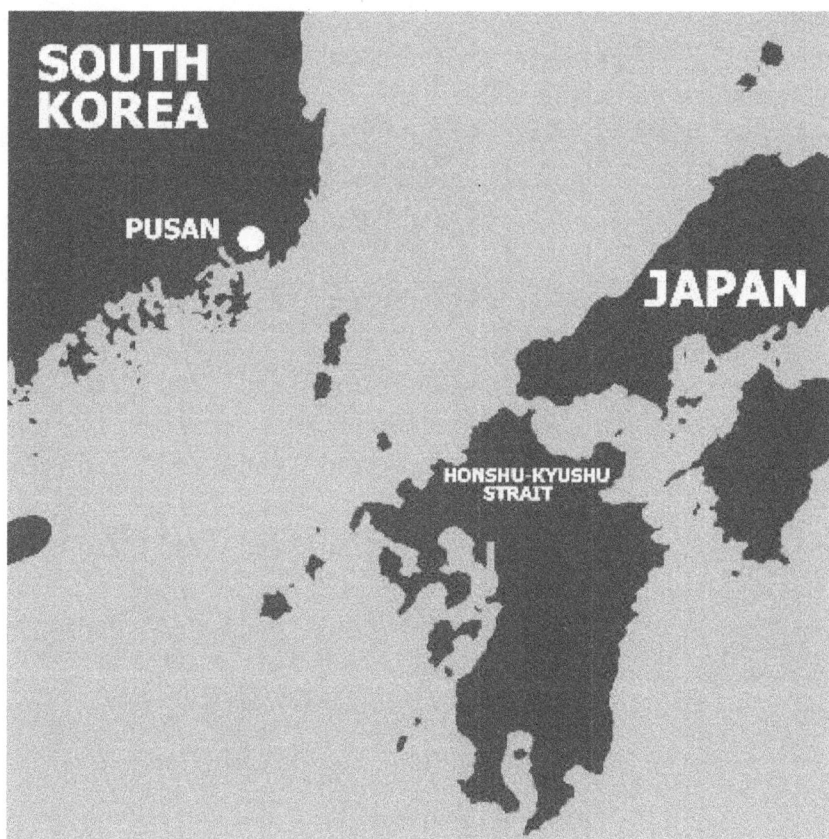

Voyage to PUSAN

back again, especially when it was so hot to drive. Thank him for me and tell him I certainly appreciate it. He's mighty good to take care of you and John for me.

In YOKOHAMA, I took a detail off the ship to go in and buy supplies for the troops in the central PX [post exchange (military commissary)] in downtown YOKOHAMA.

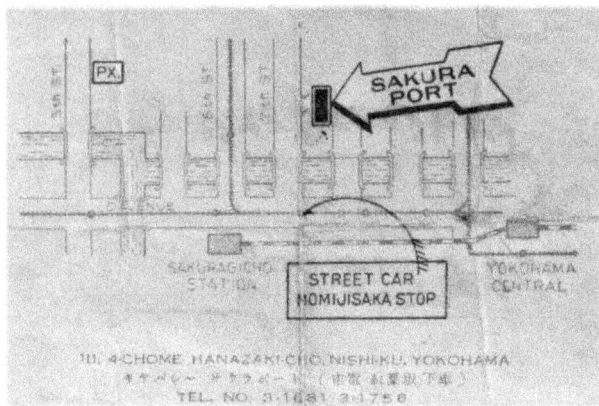

Beer hall near the PX in YOKOHAMA

This in itself proved to be quite an ordeal. The city is picturesque and literally covered with masses of humanity, all of them jabbering and going their respective ways. Anyway, with the aid of a map and a local yokel that I could hardly understand, I found the main PX. Well, if you can imagine A. Harris and Co. in the orient, you have a good idea of what I ran into. Gosh, this is the biggest one I've ever seen—everything you can imagine for sale at PX prices. You could furnish a house in about a day of buying. The reason being that so many American families live in this area. They really have it made.

I mailed a package to you there. If there is anything you want or can think of that you might want, just say so and I'll try and pick it up somewhere. I saw some beautiful block prints (wood cuts) on parchment that were nice and I plan to pick some of them up when I pass back through.

I'm stripped now of all my gear except my transport pack and weapons. Left my clothing roll in Kobe, Japan so we are ready to move out. We don't hear much about the peace talks which will begin tomorrow, but of course rumors are all over the place. No matter what happens, I believe I'll be here until the division moves out. If they can just get this thing settled, it will certainly be a relief for everyone. We are now eating field rations, and my bathtub is my hat; however, it is not so bad when you look at the poor pagan devils around you. I can't help but feel sorry for them.

I am enclosing an article that I just read in the new *Reader's Digest*. This article just about sums up my ideas and thoughts concerning a father towards his boy. Read it. It's good. I hope this letter finds you and John and everyone well. I'm doing fine.

Love you,

Your husband,
Al

When Dad referred to "division," he was talking about the 1st Marine Division out of Camp Pendleton, California. Division orders were from the highest level of Marine Corps command in Korea. The next level of command was a regiment. Dad was a part of the 11th Marine Regiment, which consisted of the 1st, 2nd, 3rd, and 4th Marine Artillery Battalions. Dad was a part of the 2nd Battalion.

A Marine artillery battalion consists of military equipment and approximately 500 men commanded by a colonel. A battalion is split into three firing batteries of approximately 150 men and 6 artillery guns (Howitzers) each. Each battery is typically commanded by a captain. The colonel commands the battalion from a headquarters battery located to the rear of the three firing battery positions. Dad was a 1st lieutenant and commanded Easy Battery. Dog and Fox Batteries were the other two batteries in the 2nd Battalion. A battalion is fully mobile and will follow the infantry troops it is supporting wherever the battle takes them.

A. Harris and Company (no relation to Al) was founded in 1887 and was one of the premier department stores in Dallas, Texas. Everyone in Greenville drove to Dallas to do their major shopping. Also, note that Dad had his eye on the Japanese parchment wood cuts. He appreciated other artists' work.

Chapter 4
THE LANDING

10 JULY 1951

Dear Mary Alice,

This is just a short note to let you know what has been going on. We are still here in PUSAN, and it has been raining for the last two days. This afternoon it cleared up, so I expect we will fly out tomorrow. The plane will take us up nearly to Seoul.

The 11th draft will be leaving before long, and I've been wondering if Frank and any of the other fellows were placed in it.

I've been gone now about a month, and I've only received one letter. The reason is because we have been moving around so much. Boy, when the letters do start rolling in, I'll bet I read for a week. I've read your first letter over 8 times.

There are a number of guys coming back now from the front who are going back home. I don't believe I've ever seen so many happy men in all my life. Hope these people knock this stuff off. We can't hear any news much. I've been very wet and muddy for the past two days but I feel fine. When are you going to send me a picture of yourself? I sure want one.

Take care of John, and remember I love you two with all my heart.

Be sweet and good night,

Love,
Al
XX

P.S. I'll send my address as soon as I can.

∝✕✕⊃

Dad arrived near Seoul, most likely at the Inchon airbase, and, judging from the dates on his letters, was immediately transferred to a troop transport where he and his platoon (approximately thirty-six men) prepared for a three-hour ride up the coast. They were going to a point twelve to thirteen miles north of the 38th parallel.

Dad and his troops had trained many times for an amphibious landing. They probably used a Landing Craft, Vehicle, Personnel (LCVP) or something similar. The LCVP was very popular in WWII and was used in the Korean War as well. It was designed to hold a platoon of men. The soldiers generally entered the boat by climbing down a cargo net hung from the side of their troop transport and exited by charging down the boat's lowered bow ramp.[9] This was the real thing. It was the middle of the night when they arrived on shore, and it was the first official duty for Lieutenant Harris in the Korean War.

They had their weapons, their 782 gear, and Dad had a map and a compass. They did not expect to encounter the enemy and their mission was to make their way to the battalion, which was a significant distance inland and a difficult climb from sea level. As Dad related the story, it was fortunate because at least there was moonlight. But nothing looked like he expected it to: nothing matched his map, and the terrain was treacherous. He had thirty-five men who were depending on him to get to the battalion, and Dad was at a loss as to what to do.

As Dad related the story, it was both a sobering and terrifying moment. He somehow had to make the right decisions. Dad said a prayer and headed off, making the best judgments he could under the circumstances. It was a defining moment that I think influenced the rest of his tour of duty. Dad said that "by the grace of God" they made it.

Dog Battery location

LETTERS ADDRESSED FROM:

1ST LIEUTENANT A. G. HARRIS

DOG BATTERY, 2ND BATTALION, 11TH MARINES

1ST MARINE DIVISION

FLEET POST OFFICE

SAN FRANCISCO, CALIFORNIA

Chapter 5
DOG BATTERY

13 JULY 1951
FRIDAY

Dear Mary Alice,

I am now located in Dog Battery, 2nd Battalion, 11th Marines. I've been up here on the lines for two days now. From our position, we can see a hill that is occupied by the enemy. Our battery is approximately 12 to 13 miles north of the 38th parallel. By what towns, I don't know. One reason is that my map is in Kobe, Japan with my clothing roll. As soon as I can find a map, I'll try to locate my position for you. We are in support of the 1st Marine Battalion. Shell joined that outfit. They are approximately 5,000 yards to our front and are on a high ridge. The 2nd Battalion has sure been firing a lot since I have been here. We are shooting day and night. I haven't been assigned to a job yet, because in about three days, I believe we will go in reserve some 20 miles back. The colonel said we (the replacements) could work into the battery there. Expect we will stay in reserve for about a month. Maybe this thing will be over by then. If this thing keeps going on, I imagine my first job will be FO, because everyone out here has spent some time as a forward observer. You see, they keep rotating them every so often. The day before I got here, they sure took a beating around the battalion with counter battery fire. Right now, the Chinese must be up to something because everyone has started opening up. My battery commander is Captain Stubbs. He seems like a nice guy and reminds you a lot of Davis—about the same build, etc. We have a Korean boy about 20 years old here in the battery with us. He acts as houseboy and also as our interpreter. He understands English better than he can speak it. We are up in the mountains and believe me, it sure gets cool at night. Last night, I was in the ex's pit (executive officer's pit) until 2400. I hit the sack about 2405 and sure had to pile the covers on.

The draft is now broken up and has been sent to many different units. Jones and Adamson are going to observe for the KMC [Korean Marine Corps]. They are on our right flank for about 2 miles. That's sure a tough job. MA, what I have just written may be a little fouled up, but it is sometimes a little hard to think straight.

Today has been a little quiet except for 4 rounds that landed far in front of us.

The country around here is some of the prettiest I've seen. It reminds me of pictures I have seen of Colorado. There is no snow on the mountaintops, but they are covered with pine. The pine here is not like East Texas pine, but is small and scrubby—very few tall ones.

The valley we are in has many creeks running through the area. The fellows in each battery have dammed up a place and have their own swimming pool. I went swimming yesterday afternoon, and it sure made me feel good. Needless to say, I didn't need a bathing suit. This may sound like we are living the Life of Riley, but nothing would suit anyone any better than to be back in the good old USA.

There is a battalion order that all personnel will wear helmets and be armed at all times. Sure glad I brought this pistol, because everyone out here wears one. I don't have to carry my carbine with me all the time.

Honey, I want to get this letter off as soon as I can so you will have my correct address. So I'll stop for now and write again maybe tomorrow.

Be sweet sweetheart,

I love you,

Al
XX

❦

After eight years of military service, and countless hours of training, Dad finally arrived at the battlefront. I can only imagine the adrenaline rush he must have had. But it appeared they would soon turn around and go in reserve a safe twenty miles back, and I'm sure that was a relief to Mom.

Dad thought his first job would be as a forward observer (FO). Around the fourth or fifth grade, Dad explained to me the whole concept of firing artillery shells. He stressed the importance of the FO, and I understood that FOs called back the position where the artillery shell hit. But the fact that they did it with a wireless radio was what really intrigued me. That was real Buck Rogers stuff back in the late '50s.

Forward observers had to be able to work independently for long periods of time, frequently behind enemy lines. It was both a dangerous and extraordinarily important job for the success of the battery, as would be proven in the months to come. The primary method of adjusting the fire was called a Grid Mission, where the FO and the artillery battery each had a grid map of the surrounding terrain. The FO would report the grid where the shell landed, adjustments would be made, and another round would be fired.[10] Once the 105 Howitzer was locked onto the target, the command would be given to "fire for effect." This typically released all six (6) gun crews to fire until the mission was complete.

From topological maps, it appears that the altitude at their position was 2,500 to 3,000 feet, so that may have had something to do with Dad saying, "It was a little hard to think straight." Or perhaps it was just a part of getting used to war.

Before Dad left for Korea, Mom bought him a brand new Smith & Wesson (S & W) .38 special, six-shot revolver to take with him. It was an authorized military pistol for use in the war. I think Mom and Dad wanted to make sure Dad had a 100-percent reliable firearm with no wear and tear. I also think the cowboy in Dad may have liked walking around with a six-shooter on his hip.

Dad was also issued a Colt .45 semi-automatic pistol by the Marine Corps, but his S & W had great stopping power and was far safer and more reliable. I believe the S & W was his primary sidearm, but Dad said that many nights he slept holding a pistol in each hand and crossed his arms over his chest.

Dad is pictured with his standard-issue M1 carbine on the cover of this book. It was an easy-to-use semi-automatic rifle that had a 15-round magazine. Used extensively in WWII and the Korean War, the M1 gained generally high praise for its small size, light weight, and firepower. Unfortunately, it also gained a reputation in Korea for jamming in sub-zero temperatures.[11]

Smith & Wesson Model 10 .38 special, 6-shot revolver

M1911 Colt .45 semi-automatic, 7-round magazine

M1 carbine, .30 caliber, semi-automatic, 15-round magazine

⌒✕✕⌒

20 JULY 1951

Dear Mary Alice,

I felt so bad lately about not writing you, but it's just one of those things that couldn't be helped. You see, starting last Sunday morning about 11:00 AM, one of the biggest artillery battles that the 11th Marines have had, started. Well, you might say it started Saturday night about 11:30 PM while I was on watch in the battery. Approximately at 11:00 PM, I got a call from battalion saying the KMC were under counter attack, and that I was to prepare the guns in order to shoot 400 mills to the right of our right safety limits. We got all squared away to try and make a stand, but nothing ever happened. Now again on Sunday morning things began popping. We started getting rounds right in the battery area. They were from 4 artillery guns the Gooks had set up way in the distance. We had about 100 rounds land in the area. Seven men were hit by shrapnel but none too seriously. Captain Stubbs was hit under his left eye, that made a deep cut. He felt very lucky that he didn't lose it. We all had some very close shaves that day, but your old husband came through without even a small cut. I was sure lucky. We had an advantage that saved many a man's life. It was this—at first by straining your ears you could hear the Gook guns go off, and then in about 15 seconds you would hear them come whistling in. Note that I said "at first" we had to strain to hear them go off. Well, after about the first six landed, I don't believe there was a man in the battery that couldn't hear the commands [gun shots] as they were loading them up. We sure did act like gophers there for a long time. Ha Ha!

Monday we were to be relieved by an Army unit. I started getting 3 trucks and 2 jeeps packed up with gear to move back to an assembly area. I was to move out by 1200 that day, and the captain was to bring the rest of the battery at 1800. Well, just as I left out with my convoy, the Gooks must have seen us, because here they came with those shells again. The battery was under fire the rest of the day. I took the convoy back to the assembly area and had tents set up along with the galley. I started supper, and waited for the battery to come on in at 1800. They made it OK without anyone hurt. Out of the assembly area, we moved some 30 miles to the rear, and I am now in reserve. We are set up and living in tents that are full of shrapnel holes. It is raining now and I don't have a stitch of dry clothes. We have been out in the area all day digging drainage ditches so the place won't be flooded. Last night's rain brought the water about 6 inches in every tent. We have it all ditched now, along with a sand floor that we got off the creek.

21 JULY 1951

I was so tired last night that I had to stop on the third page of this letter. So, I'll finish this morning. First of all, the peace talks don't sound very good. Seems that this thing will go on and on. Maybe the next three days will tell. John will soon have a birthday. I sure wish I could be there to see him and have a party, but that is far from possible. Give him a big hug, and tell him that his daddy loves him very much. This is the month for a lot of birthdays in our family—tell them all happy birthday for me.

I should be getting some mail now in a day or two. As of yet, your first letter has been the only one. Bet it will take me a long time to catch up reading them. It is the rainy season here, and all the creeks and rivers around here are busy rushing their loads of water away. The food we have been getting in is very good and well prepared. I am well, but believe I am losing a little weight.

Honey, I love you always.

Be sweet,

Albert
XX

⚬⟨⟩⚬

Dad was starting to see some serious combat action and hadn't had an opportunity to write Mom for a week. He probably assumed his letters were getting out, and yet he had been there for over a month and had only received one letter from Mom. What he didn't know was that regular mail was not yet established in either direction, so Mom was in the same boat.

In the letter, Dad makes his first reference to "Gooks." It is a derogatory name for Southeast Asians, especially enemy soldiers. It can be traced to the early twentieth century but gained widespread notice as a result of the Korean and Vietnam wars.[12] Conversely, Koreans viewed Americans as stupid and ignorant—as thinking they have everything and are more advanced. They called us "American Hamburgers" (frankly, I'm not too offended by that).[13]

I have no tolerance for racial slurs, derogatory names, or offensive talk of any sort. It has no place in today's world. However, soldiers have been demeaning the enemy since the beginnings of war, and I think they always will.

On a related subject, after WWII one the first mass-marketed products from Japan was rubber "flip-flops" or "thong" shoes. In the mid 1950s, I remember seeing them stacked up in the department stores. They were inexpensive and we all bought a pair. I loved wearing them in the summer and around our house, they were simply known as "Gook" shoes. I didn't know any different and never thought a thing about it.

23 JULY 1951

Dear Mary Alice,

Today is my birthday, and yesterday I got one of the most wonder-ful birthday presents I've ever had—this was three letters from you. Gosh, I've waited and waited, but as each day went by and I didn't get any, I knew they were stacking up somewhere and that a good day was on its way. They couldn't have arrived at a more opportune time. I noticed you said nothing about mail from me. I believe by the time you get this letter, you should have all of my previous letters, and our mail should be steady. The fellows say it takes around seven days. Honey, don't send any more stamps unless I ask you to, because they stick together by the time they go over all that water.

Back here in reserve, we have a tent set up for PX gear. Yesterday I bought myself this $1.50 pen I'm writing with, a pipe, and a can of orange juice (cooled it in the creek and drank it today). Who could ask for a better birthday party! Tonight we had a special service show. It was made up entirely of service men from an army special service platoon. It was called "Take Ten." The words "take ten" are frequently used to signify that you have a 10-minute break in whatever you're doing. The show was good and had many musical numbers along with much comedy and burlesque; however, the cast was made up of entirely of men. Gives a fellow a good time to see a show once every now and then.

Baby, it's bedtime, so I will finish this tomorrow sometime. Sleep tight. I love you.

24 JULY 1951

Today I've been working on a lecture that I will give this Friday on mines and booby traps. I've sure learned a lot about enemy weapons. Sure hope this Wednesday will bring about a peace settlement; however, the talk around here is doubtful. We didn't get any mail today, so you can see I'm about ready to get another battalion mail orderly.

The weather around here the last few days has been sunny and very hot. Reminds me very much of Greenville weather. Around here we bathe in a small creek that runs into the river. The creek is about 300 yards from my tent. The water is cold, and it takes some time to get accustomed to it. Tomorrow, we will go out in the field on an RSOP (reconnaissance, selection, and occupation of position). The problems are very much the same as the ones we ran at Pendleton. Have to hit the sack now. Love you.

∝⋙∘

26 JULY 1951

Mary Alice,

I've tried for the past two days to finish this letter but have found no time for it. Today I went on a 35-mile ride to an ammo dump to collect mines for my lecture tomorrow. They sure keep us busy with odd jobs of some sort. I'm now assistant executive officer of Dog Battery, and will become executive when Hillshire leaves in about one month. I think this will be fine, and sure hope I can hold down the job. Baby, I'll quit now, but will write again soon.

Love, your Marine

AL, XX

P. S. I have to make up some notes now.

∞✖∞

Dad had his master's degree and was an experienced math teacher. He was always a good speaker, and I imagine his superior officers were taking note of his abilities. There is no doubt that he put on a highly informative and entertaining lecture on Korean land mines, complete with a variety of visual aids.

∞✖∞

SUNDAY
29 JULY 1951

Dear Mary Alice,

Today I received much mail from home. Right now, I am fit to be tied. You will never know how happy a letter makes me feel. I wish very much your money from the Marine Corps would start coming in; however, I guess that it will in due time. I have on the books here $220 and will send that on to you as soon as we are paid. This may be several months though. Your job at Lance sounds good. Baby, I know it will be hard for you to work and leave John, but I do have faith in your feelings and I know you will do the right thing. I'm very proud of my little girl you see. I am so glad you liked the things I sent from Japan. Maybe someday soon I will send more.

I now have a new job, and I hope I can do it. You see, Easy (E) Battery's commander (Captain Batson) is going home on rotation. This leaves that battery without a commanding officer. So, the wheels got together and decided that I am the one to take the job over. This is a captain's job, but there are none in the battalion at present. I figure that when a captain does come in, I will be relieved and take other duties elsewhere. But as it now stands, I will be Easy Battery commander at 0800 tomorrow morning. This is the biggest job I've ever had in the Marine Corps. I will have eight officers, 150 men, six 105 Howitzers, 13 trucks (6 x 6), two jeeps, and gosh only knows how much other material.

Model M101
105 mm Howitzer

As the situation now stands (WAR), we are getting ready to support a push by the Korean Marine Corps. We haven't been given a jump-off date but as things look it won't be long. So, your husband may take Easy Battery into combat. If we are committed, I will take it as a very wonderful honor to lead these fine men. Most of the men are young but good in their jobs. I've promised myself that I will do everything in my power to guide and direct them, and with God's help I know I will be successful. The peace talks have sounded very good for the past few days, but today not so good. The army unit that relieved us is sure taking a beating. Hope they can at least hold.

I'm sure getting a lot of sun here, so much in fact I would say I am very brown. Many of the boys around here are so black you can hardly tell them from the natives.

Tomorrow we will all go out and re-zero our weapons. We sure want them so we can hit something if necessary.

Today or tomorrow is John's birthday, and I know he will have a happy one. Get the little fella a lot of toys, because boys his age sure need them.

Love, Al XX

P.S. In my address just change D to E.

I have a few minutes more before the movie starts, so I'll write some more (you wouldn't want your old man to miss a show though). Tell Lila that if she wants some pictures, I will be glad to pick them up for her. Also, see if she has a color preference and I'll try and get them.

Today, we built a dam in the creek, and now we have a fine swimming hole to cool off in. There are many deer in the area—we see many signs and I have seen several myself. The warrant officer in our tent has killed lots. Maybe I'll get one before long.

Love, Al

⚬⚬⚬

So, forty-three days from getting on board the USS **William Weigel,** *Dad assumed command of a Marine artillery battery and had over 150 men reporting to him. There were very few 1ˢᵗ lieutenants holding that position, and he was preparing to go into combat. I'm sure Dad attacked the job with tireless effort and professional enthusiasm; he would have the best artillery battery in the battalion. You can see his genuine concern for the men he would lead, and that would continue throughout his tour of duty.*

He had six (6) 105 mm Howitzers that weighed 5,000 pounds each. They fired a 4.1" diameter, thirty-three-pound shell a maximum distance of seven miles. The shell itself had a thirty-three-yard kill radius on impact. They were ideal for supporting ground troops and could easily be towed behind a 6 x 6 (6-wheel drive) heavy-duty truck.[14]

On a humorous note, Dad had two Jeeps that were assigned to his battery. One of them was his personal Jeep. With all the different types of equipment that the battalion had, vehicle maintenance was a constant issue. In Dad's battery, it seems they had a number of soldiers who happened to be excellent car mechanics as well. Regardless of a lack of spare parts, Dad said his Jeep was always in top running condition. He wasn't sure, but there might have been some late-night swapping of parts from other Jeeps in the battalion!

LETTERS ADDRESSED FROM:

1ST LIEUTENANT A. G. HARRIS

EASY BATTERY, 2ND BATTALION, 11TH MARINES

1ST MARINE DIVISION

FLEET POST OFFICE

SAN FRANCISCO, CALIFORNIA

Chapter 6
EASY BATTERY

5 AUG. 1951

Dear Mary Alice and John,

Last night I received five letters; three from you and two from my mother. Two of your letters were written recently; however, one was postmarked June 28. It told me of your trip home, how the car stood up, the payment you made, etc. I believe I now have all of your back letters and will start receiving them regularly. The clipping you sent about John being in the mock wedding sure sounded cute, and I know he and Wynn put on a show for you. Thanks for the picture—it is viewed quite often by the fellows passing my tent.

6 AUG. 1951

Mary Alice, I've been trying to write this letter for the past three days, but it seems that as a battery commander, you have very little time to relax. We have been out shooting all day. We are now losing many of the old men that made the Inchon landing and are receiving many new men to take their place.

In my battery, we have six 105 Howitzers that have a personality all their own now. You see, the other day Lieutenant Winger, my XO (executive offier [second in command]), said the gun crews were sure wanting to name their pieces, but they had no way of painting the names on them. So, you can guess the rest—yes, their battery commander painted them. Here are the names and each is very appropriate for their duty.

Gun 1 – Screaming Death
Gun 2 – Honey Pot Buster
Gun 3 – Gook Lullaby
Gun 4 – Chink Scrambler
Gun 5 – Baloo Undertaker
Gun 6 – Slopehead Slaughterer

Some of the words might be foreign to you, so I'll try and explain. "Honey pot" are the words used for an air outdoor toilet, and "Baloo" is Korean for Chinese communist. You would be surprised to see how such little things affect the morale of the troops.

Honey, we are now on a definite standby for August 15. We will move out sometime around that date. I have no idea where we will go, but the division has requested we have all our gear fixed so we can load it aboard ship. Now this doesn't mean we are going to sea, because it is just paperwork and planning. Could be a landing in the making, or it might even be that the whole 1st Marines would leave Korea. Now this is strictly pipe dreaming on my part, because as far as I know, we will move back up in the line. Next week, we will go out and fire for the 2nd Battalion 1st Marines and also the KMC.

Today, one man in my battery had $120 stolen from him while he was out in the field. Now I've got an investigation on my hands. I don't think I can do very much about it, but I just have no patience with a person that leaves money lying around.

Tell John that the birthday card I received from him was super and his note was the cutest I've ever read—but that handwriting had a look about it. Ha! Ha! Sure appreciated the card from your folks too. Mother sent me one with pictures of the farm, all the dogs, etc. You know they have another batch don't you?

In the morning, we have seven officers leaving for the States. Boy are they happy. Someday soon, I hope I'll get to make that trip. The movie tonight is *Jolson Sings Again*. Remember when we saw it there at the Texan?

Baby, from what I can hear from the other fellows and comparing my allotment (to you) to theirs, I should be keeping on the books about $90 per month. Tell you what I'll do. Believe I'll just let it accumulate until I leave and perhaps we can have a small amount saved up. Now that is if you don't need it. If you do just say so and when I'm paid again, I'll get it in a check and mail it to you.

This is one place I take a bath every day (down at Bare Bottom Beach)—everything is so dusty. I don't believe there is a paved road in Korea. The sun is doing me good except last Sunday I stayed a little while too long at Bare Bottom and boy was my bottom red. You know, I'm peeling off there right now.

I haven't written my folks for some time now. Please write them and tell them I'm OK. As soon as I can, I'll get a letter off.

There are a number of very nice officers here in camp in the battalion. One you may remember went to artillery school at Quantico with me—Jim Shea. His wife now lives in Oceanside—too bad we didn't know that. Some of the fellows coming in the 11th draft say it is so big that it took three ships to bring them across. The 1st is to be as big or bigger.

Well, honey, I've just written down things as they popped into my mind so I expect you may have a hard time figuring them out. Baby, I miss you so, I just long at times to hold you in my arms for even a few seconds. Good night, sweetheart, and I love you.

Your Marine,

AL XX

Take care of John.

P.S. There are many funny sayings that come out of situations like this, and from time to time I will write some of them to you.

Here is what we call a roll of toilet paper:

1. Head Tape
2. Music Roll
3. Daily News

… and many others.

⌁⌁⌁

Dad had a unique opportunity for his creative talent to help him bond with his troops. Can you imagine their surprise when the commanding officer came out and started painting the names on the Howitzers? Dad was an expert in lettering with anything from a pen to a brush. I guarantee you each of those guns had a name and a personality all their own. I would be very surprised if each did not have its own graphics as well. Apparently it had a very positive effect on troop morale.

Dad also mentions the "Texan." It was a classic old movie theater in downtown Greenville, Texas, and I saw a lot of movies there growing up. I remember that some of the older boys would light paper matches and throw them off the balcony during the movie—pure 1950s mischief!

11 AUG. 1951

Dear Mary Alice and John,

Honey, I just got your picture that you sent in my birthday card. I remember that day I took it—you were so pretty and sweet. Gosh honey, I just love you something awful. I think of you and John every day and each day that goes by makes me want to see you more than ever. Thanks so much. There is nothing that I wanted more.

Sorry you are having trouble with the pay office at Oceanside—tell you what you do though, mail me the letter you got from them and I think I can square it away. Also, Colonel Edwards of the 10th draft is just up the way. Maybe I can go and see him if nothing else can be done.

The seat covers for the car sound good, and gosh I know we needed them. I can hardly wait to see the sample you are sending. I'll bet you made a good choice.

Your husband has been working very hard for the past week trying to get Easy Battery squared away. We are losing more of the old men who have been with the battery since Inchon. Makes it very rough trying to make them work like a team.

This next week we will do a lot of shooting for the KMC and also for the 1st Marines. I believe Lieutenant Jones and Lieutenant Adams will be spotting naval gunfire for them. Hope I get to see them.

Baby, you may think this is a poor thing to do, but I'm going to do it anyway. I'm planning to buy a movie camera and also a projector. I've looked some over that I've seen and they sure look good to me. It will be more than likely an 8 mm. If I do buy them, I think I'll keep the camera and send you the projector. Then I'll take movies and send them home to you. We could also use it with John. Write and tell me what you think of this idea. I've always wanted one, and now seems an opportune time to get it with things much cheaper here. When I say here, I mean in Japan. My friend Jim Tucker is there now, and he will do the job for me if and when I decide to go through with it.

I got a letter from Uncle Les telling about your coming by on the way home. He said that John was sure cute and he went straight for the candy jar.

⊂⟨⟩⊃

In this letter, Dad approached Mom with the idea of buying a movie camera and projector. It wouldn't be his last correspondence on the subject.

⊂⟨⟩⊃

13 AUG. 1951

Baby, I've sure been hustling around here taking Easy Battery for shoots. We assimilated naval gunfire for the 1st Battalion 1st Marines today. Last night during the movie, a boy accidentally shot himself with a carbine. He was hit in the right side of his chest. The doctor was to him approximately 1 ½ minutes after it happened. He will live, but boy it was close. Seems like trouble always comes in bunches. Today, two large trucks hit as they were going around the mountain, and one of them went over the side some 50 feet below.

Luckily, the boys were thrown clear and not hurt too seriously. The other night during a big rain, our showers that we had set up by the river washed down. Was the colonel ever mad! I just got through with a bath down at "Bare Bottom Beach." Sure makes a fella feel good. Baby, I'm very tired, so I'll write you again when I can. Take care of John. Your Marine loves you as ever.

Albert XX

∝✕✕⊃

SUNDAY 19 AUG. 1951

Dear Mary Alice,

Right now, your husband is having a lot of trouble but perhaps I can get it squared away soon. First of all, yesterday afternoon I told my 1st sergeant to send out a detail to cut some logs for our battery area. Well, they went out and took a 6 x 6 GMC [General Motors Corporation] truck. Up on a mule trail about 1 ½ miles off the MSR (main supply route), the road gave way and the truck is now down in a gully upside down. What a headache I have now trying to salvage that hunk of gear. On top of this, one of my corpsmen went AWOL [absent without leave] and was picked up in Won Ju in a cat house. I will have to take him up to see the colonel tomorrow morning. I will recommend a summary court. I hate to do this to the boy, but we must have reliable people in this area.

I have good news about our staying here in reserve. Our training schedule has now been extended to the 17th of September. But up in front of us, they have been in the attack and are getting hit hard. The

Army Division is known over here as the "bug out" artist, and we are expecting to move out at any time. This is based on the proposition that the army has to move out. The peace talks sound good, and perhaps this thing can be temporarily settled or maybe for good.

I will go up and see Colonel Edwards this afternoon and have the copy of the Certificate in Lieu of Orders made up. I will mail it in another envelope separately. It is sure nice to get mail from you. I know I haven't been writing as I should, but things are sure keeping me busy.

Enjoyed the letter from Mr. McCollom, but for your information only, he can do fairly well on those topics he discussed and we realize the situation to the fullest. If you see him, tell him thanks and I appreciate the advice.

I've been trying to build a road through our battery area to the MSR but here lately we've had so much rain, it's been rather difficult to place a foundation that will last. Anyway, we keep the CAT's [Caterpillar tractors] working.

This Marine Corps can sure keep a guy fouled up sometimes with their changing of ways. They sure messed Cloyce Box up didn't they.

Honey, I would like for you to mail me a little notebook and also a stencil pen that I could mark clothes with. I would like 4 (four) notebooks. We can't get any over here, and I sure need some. Would also like to have about two spiral pads to refill my leather folder. If you can get this, please airmail it.

Honey, I think of you and John all the time, and I hope you are well and having fun. Please don't hurt your toe anymore. I know you were good at things like that. Better run and mail this.

I love you,

Al XX

⚯

The Certificate in Lieu of Orders was a document that Mom needed to file for travel reimbursement for the trip Offie took to Camp Pendleton to move Mom and me back to Greenville.

Cloyce Box was an American football player and businessman. He played five years in the National Football League with the Detroit Lions and was a member of NFL championship teams in 1952 and 1953. In February 1951, Box was recalled from inactive reserve status by the U.S. Marine Corps and missed the entire 1951 NFL season.[15]

Dad was always very organized, and Mom supplied him with the pads he requested, but they wouldn't get there for a while.

20 AUG. 1951

Dear Mary Alice,

Honey, I just got this copy of the Certificate in Lieu of Orders from Colonel Edwards himself and he has signed it. This will make it our original even though it is a copy by certification. I'm also sending two copies so you can forward them all, and this should do the job. My battery is on notice to move out in 30 minutes. Believe this will not be a problem though. I've got to hurry. Will write again soon.

Al, XX

Chapter 7
THE FRONT

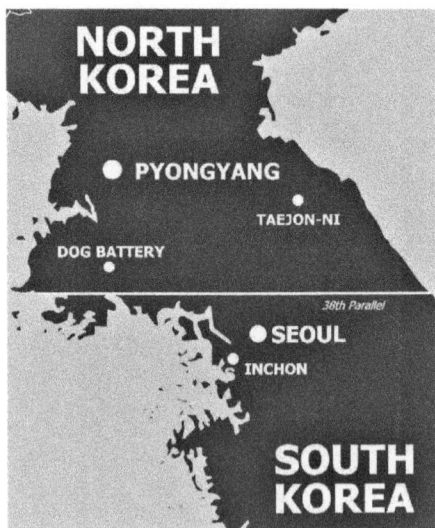

Location of TAEJON-NI

Dear Mary Alice,

Honey, I haven't written you in a long time, so I've made up my mind that today I would write a very long letter; it may be sometime before I can write again. We are moving back up front probably Tuesday. We have been in the Central Area and will now move over to the East Coast, somewhere in the area of TAEJON-NI.

I don't know if you will be able to pick these places out on your map, but we will be as far as our lines have advanced on the east front and about 25 to 30 miles off the coast of the Sea of Japan. Since the peace talks have fallen through, we are expecting the next two months to bring much fighting from both sides. The days are getting cool here in August, and by November it is said that it will be so cold it will be hard for both sides to move. So, standby for the next two months.

Dad at TAEJON-NI

Now MA, I want you to understand that what I'm about to say is for your own good. So, you will have to take it as it comes. If by any chance that I am hit at any time, the Red Cross will wire you and my family at the same time. So please take it with a grain of salt, because it may not be as bad as it sounds. I just don't want you to be alarmed unduly. If this ever happens, you can bet I'll let you know the particulars by mail as soon as I can.

This afternoon, I will have all my trucks and jeeps sandbagged. This may come in handy sometime.

This job as battery commander sure keeps me jumping, and there are many heartaches that go along with it. You see, I have to decide many times as to which men will go home. And there are times I have to tell them they can't go because we have no replacements. Now believe me, it hits hard to have that job. The word is out about our moving up, so we can expect many men to inflict wounds on themselves rather than go back. It's hell to try and keep things running smoothly.

I got three letters from you yesterday. I can hardly wait until I get the pictures you promised. So glad your toe is better. If I haven't made a comment about your living on Sayle Street, it was certainly unintentional. I thought that I had. I think it's swell and I know it's best for you and John. Baby, as soon as I am paid, I will send you $200. I have requested to be paid by check. I will mail it to you with no endorsement and I believe you can take care of it at the bank, can't you? I have lost count on how much you have paid on the car. Apply all you can without denying yourself anything. I will still have $119 on the books, so you can see I will be all right. We have no need for money at all. We get a lot of candy in our PX ration, but sometime you might send me some nuts in cans—they sure are good. I have enough stationery to last about two weeks if I write a lot, so don't send any until I say so.

I now have two new sets of dungarees, a new cap, a new pair of shoes and an air mattress. So, you can see I'm all fixed up on gear fairly well. Seems that I told you about the truck that was lost in the mountains.

Well, I had it surveyed and we now have a new 6 x 6. Also, a new Jeep. Our gun section (Baloo Undertaker) was pretty well worn—also had it surveyed and now I have a new Howitzer.

Baby, I will probably make captain on the next list out, so we may make some money on that deal because they date them back. I will receive that difference for the months that I have been paid as a 1st lieutenant. It probably won't be much, but maybe it will help.

The fellow that I recommended for a summary court martial will be tried sometime today. As I told you, I sure hate to do things like that but sometimes it can't be helped.

I now have a Korean interpreter in the battery. His name is YU. He seems like a good worker and speaks English fairly well. When he came to the battery, he had only the clothes on his back so I outfitted him with a change and you could sure tell he was happy. Baby, I must get busy now and get ready to go. There's a lot to do, so be sweet and remember I will always love you. You and John have a good time.

Love from your Marine.

Al XX

I see that I still have a little more time so I'll continue to write. Last night I went to a stage show at the 1st Engineering Battalion about a mile north of here. It was a USO [United Service Organization] show with only four girls. They sure put on a show—all good clean fun. Of course, they were scantily dressed, which made the fellas go wild. The mistress of ceremony was very clever and did many imitations of well-known Hollywood actors and actresses. One of her best was Bette Davis—you know that stance she has. We all had field glasses and took the show in well.

I got a letter from Uncle Les a while back so if you see him tell him thanks and as soon as I have time, I will drop him a line. You sure have been knocking yourself out writing everyone. You are mighty sweet to do so and I know everyone will appreciate it. I've also received two letters from my aunt Alice (in Eddy). It is certainly nice of her to write but I can't be writing all the time to try to keep up. Please mention in one of your letters to Mother that I have gotten them.

Baby, I'll see you.

Love, Al XX

∞§∞

It had been four weeks since Dad took over command of Easy Battery. They had been in reserve, training and getting ready to move to the front. The time had come for Dad to inform Mom that the chances he would be wounded in battle were about to increase substantially. He made a valiant effort at low-keying it by telling Mom "to take things with a grain of salt" if she got a telegram from the Red Cross. Dad was always an optimist.

Helen Meyer worked at the Johnson Air Force Hospital in Japan where many wounded Marines were transferred. On February 18, 1951, she wrote in a letter to her parents:

"Because there are so many self-inflicted wounds it just shows the lack of spirit there is in this war. So many of the boys will do anything to get out of Korea. They will even tear open their own wounds at night in the hospitals here in Japan and hold their thermometers under matches to keep from going back to duty."[16]

⚭

SEPT 1, 1951

Dear Mary Alice and John,

Honey, I haven't written you lately simply because I have been so busy with these damn Gooks. Just want you to know I am well and doing great. All my boys are OK too.

This morning we knocked out two companies of Gooks. I was up-front looking for a new position and could see through my field glasses what we were doing—ran the rest back.

I received John's pictures you sent. Baby, they are swell. He sure has grown a lot.

Baby, I must stop for now, because we will be moving up soon. This time we will be in the area around the village of HABAEYANG.

Remember I love you!

Your Marine,

Al

✑

There was no date on the following letter. It was written in a big hurry on a scrap piece of notepaper. Dad's writing was uncharacteristically sloppy. The envelope was dated Sept 6, so it was probably written on the 4ᵗʰ. Something big was brewing.

✑

Dear Mary Alice,

I am now back in division getting some scope on something coming up soon. You'll read about it in the newspapers. We will be moving out soon. Will write more when I get time.

This letter also has a $200 check.

Your last letter was in one of the rivers over here for some time. The mail truck was hijacked.

Love, Al

(over)

I'm doing OK—I love you.

SUNDAY SEPT. 9, 1951

Dear Mary Alice and John,

Right now, your old man is below HUDONG-NI, and we are set up on the slope of a hill that has springs all over the place. With so many springs, you can imagine how muddy the place is. I have only written you two short notes since we were committed. Up until now, this is the first breathing space we have had. We have been behind the 7th Marines supporting the KMC that are on the left flank of the 7th. I just saw Dick Shell. He had a company during the heaviest fighting around here—he lost 17 men out of his outfit; however, he made it out without a scratch. You feel very lucky sometimes. I asked him to stay and have chow, but as he was in a hurry, he couldn't.

I haven't yet received my notebooks, and I suspect very much they are lost. You see, the other day the mail trucks were hijacked and they took all the packages—dumping the mail in the river. One of your letters was salvaged, but it had sure been underwater. I hope my books were not taken but they may have been.

About this business I mentioned in my note with the check, there are big doings that will come off very soon, and perhaps you'll read about it. I can't say any more now, but later on I'm sure the whole thing will be revealed.

The weather here is beginning to turn cold, and it won't be long until we are issued our winter gear. I'm now having to sleep under two blankets as well as my sleeping bag. I know you must be having a terrible time with the heat. So take care, and you and John play it cool.

We have been getting in a number of replacements in enlisted status as well as officers. This is good because many of the men are very tired. I sure like to see a man go home when his time is up.

I got a lot of pictures from Mother the other day. It is surprising to see the progress that has been made on the house. You mentioned that you might like to send me a package of Lance stuff. I think that would be swell, if you have time. I would like it, and I know the other fellows would too. There are so many Lance products, so I think they would go over big. Say, I need a flashlight too.

The pictures of our boy are the best ever. Gosh, I sure wish I could be there to play with him and some of the toys he got. Tell him that his daddy will send him something one of these days.

MA, I hope the check arrives OK. You can do anything you want with it. I was going to buy that movie camera with it but just didn't have a chance. And I figured that the U.S. mail would be as safe as it was with me. So, here's hoping it gets there.

I guess the kids are getting ready to go back to school now, and I might be going back myself if I were there. If you happen to see any of them there in Greenville, please tell them that I often think of the times we have had. The back of this page is for John. Maybe he would like a small letter once in a while.

Baby, I'll close for now and will write more some other time. We are now on the rim of the PUNCHBOWL.

I love you both.
Al

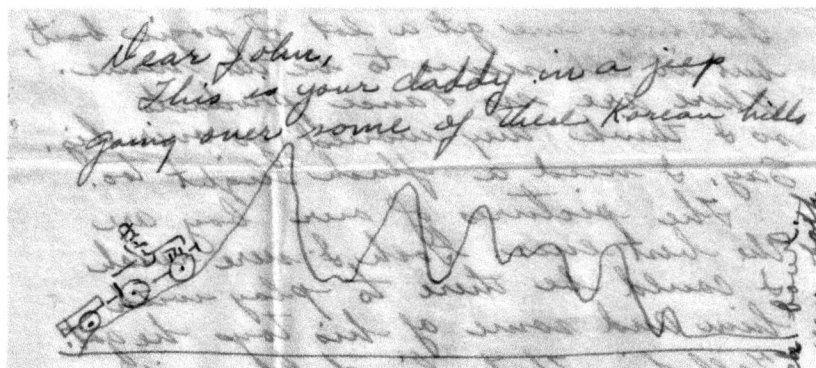

Dear John,
This is your daddy in a jeep
going over some of these Korean hills

THIS IS A KOREAN COW

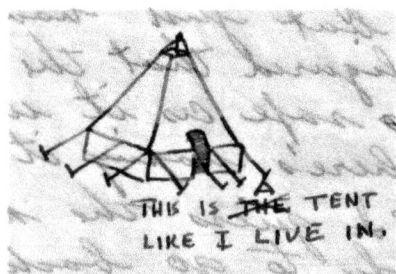

THIS IS THE TENT
LIKE I LIVE IN,

HONEY POT.

WE HAVE A LOT OF THESE IN OUR BN.

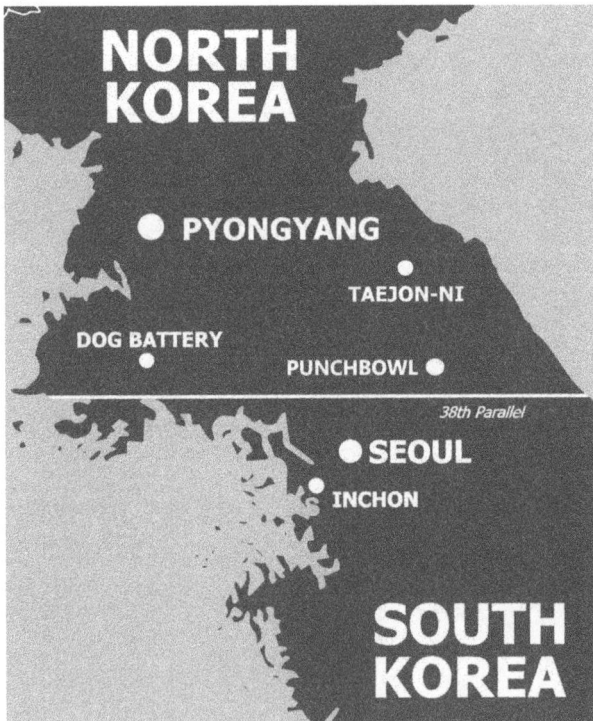

Location of the PUNCHBOWL

Chapter 8

BATTLE OF THE PUNCHBOWL

The "big doings" Dad referred to was the Battle of the Punchbowl. It lasted from approximately August 31 to September 21. This was why Dad had returned to his division on September 4 and had hastily written Mom a note. His buddy, Dick Shell, had already lost seventeen men in the early stages of the battle. The "Punchbowl" was a bowl-shaped, extinct volcano ringed by the Taebaek mountain range located approximately fifteen miles north of the 38th parallel in central North Korea.[17]

General Matthew Ridgway was the U.S. Army commander who led the UN troops in Korea in 1951. In his book, The Korean War, *he describes the fighting in the area of the Punchbowl:*

"The fighting was perhaps the bloodiest to date and the most strenuous, demanding the utmost in physical strength, endurance and raw courage. Infantrymen fought like Indians, crawling up hillsides, lugging mortar rounds as well as their own rifles and ammunition and sometimes having to blast the enemy out of dug-in positions at point-blank range. [Enemy troops] worked with Oriental doggedness to fortify [themselves] in the hills, sometimes tunneling, with hand labor, from the reverse slope of a hill, so that [they] could pull out of [their] forward positions under air and artillery attack and find shelter on the reverse slope of a hill, where it was difficult to zero in on [them] with airstrikes or heavy Howitzers. [They] might build tunnels as much as a thousand yards long to enable [them] to take quick shelter from bombardment, yet move forward to meet an attack on the ground."[18]

Following the breakdown of peace talks in August 1951, the UN Command decided to launch a limited offensive in the late summer/early autumn to shorten and straighten sections of their lines, acquire better defensive terrain, and deny the enemy key vantage points from which they could observe and target UN positions. The Battle of the Punchbowl itself consisted of two phases: (1) the battle for Yoke Ridge and (2) the battle for Kanmubong Ridge. Each of these phases consisted of many smaller violent battles for control of the numerous numbered hills in the area.[17]

On August 31, the 7th Marines and two battalions of the 1st KMC launched an attack on the eastern edge of the

Punchbowl moving toward Yoke Ridge in the west. On September 1, the 1ˢᵗ KMC moved west along Yoke Ridge, while the 7ᵗʰ Marines moved north, both assault groups clearing out KPA (Korean People's Army) bunkers with grenades and flamethrowers. Between September 4-10, the 1ˢᵗ Marines and the 1ˢᵗ KMC consolidated their positions on Yoke Ridge and built up ammunition and supplies for the second phase of the attack on Kanmubong Ridge.[17]

It was considered essential to seize Kanmubong Ridge, immediately north of Yoke Ridge, in order to attack the KPA main line of resistance, which was believed to be located approximately 2 miles north. On September 13, the 2ⁿᵈ Battalion, 1ˢᵗ Marines were ordered to seize Hill 749. Hill 749 proved to be a heavily defended fortress of bunkers, covered trenches, and tunnels and was part of the KPA main line of resistance. On September 16, the Marines seized the summit at 12:10, but were soon driven back. They finally gained control of the summit by 15:00, but it would be 20:25 before they could relieve the 2ⁿᵈ Battalion, 7ᵗʰ Marines on the reverse slope of the hill.[17]

The UN offensive in the Punchbowl area concluded on September 21; however, the KPA continued to probe the UN lines and direct fire on their positions. At the end of the UN offensive in early October, 1951, UN forces controlled the line of hills north of the Punchbowl.[17]

In a future letter dated January 20, 1952, Dad sent Mom the picture that appears on the cover of this book, with the following explanation:

Dad on Hill 749

"It seems that I have been sending you quite a few pictures of myself lately, but I just can't help it, because someone is always giving me one that they took way back then. This one, this time, was taken on approximately September 14, 1951. [He missed the date by several days.] We had just taken the hill that I am on (Hill 749). The two rifles that are slung over my left shoulder are Russian made jobs that were left by the retreating enemy. I brought them back to the battery for some of my forward observers."

Dad's account of the battle of Hill 749 is detailed in his next letter.

∞✕∞

MONDAY SEPTEMBER 17

My Dear Mary Alice and John,

At last things have slacked off enough so I can take some time to tell you what has been going on. For about three weeks now we have had one hell of a time. The past four days have been the worst of all though. For the past four days, we have been in direct support of the 1st Marine Regiment, and Easy Battery has been in support of the 2nd Battalion of that regiment. Dog and Fox have been supporting the 1st and 3rd Battalions. Well, anyway the 7th Marines were nearly wiped out trying to take two hills up here, so they were relieved and the 1st Marines passed through their lines and took over. Now, my forward observers are attached to the 2nd Battalion 1st Marines. When we started out, I had 4 officers and 23 men with them. Well, the 2nd Battalion was chosen to spearhead the attack with Easy Battery in close support. The fighting was as rough as any that the Marine Corps has ever experienced in this operation. The first day, we lost in my FO teams one officer (Lieutenant Thomas) and 13 men. I won't list them here, but I do have their names in my papers. When I received word that my teams had fallen, I asked for volunteers from the battery to go forward with me to fill up the teams. The first day I took 6 men and one officer (Lieutenant Dench) up. We reorganized our teams and continued on in the attack. I have never in my life seen so many people being slaughtered. Many of the boys were cracking up. I had one that did. We went on until dark, and when we started digging in for the night, I returned to the battery. That night there was a counterattack by the Gooks, and we fired all night long. The attack was stopped about 5:30 AM, and we hadn't given back an inch of ground. Our boys did a wonderful job, and I was especially proud of Lieutenant Laney, a little short fat guy. He was out front in a machine gun pit with two machine gunners, and all he had with him was his 6-19 radio. He was overrun that night, but he stayed right in there and called down the fire that stopped them. He will more than likely get a Silver Star out of it. He was not hit. Also, the same night, I lost Lieutenant Dench and his radio operator. They were hit by mortar fire. I spent the next day up on the hill myself with some more replacements and got to do some shooting. This time I took Lieutenant Santee and Sergeant Powell up. After getting them in position, I returned to the battery and started getting supplies for my FOs and also checking on my wounded. They were transported from the front by helicopter to an aid station. My boys were hit bad but none of them are near death. The doctor tells me they will all pull through. I got to see most of them and I hope I cheered them up some. Bless their hearts each and every one of them—they are doing a great job. I just got a message from the 2nd Battalion colonel. "We certainly think a lot of our artillery boys; they saved our hides." What we have left on the hill now is small in number, but they are there to stay, and come hell or high water they will. Well, honey, that's what we've been doing. I've been very lucky and haven't gotten a scratch as of yet. One of my good friends, Charles Dunne in Dog Battery, was hit Saturday and died early Sunday morning. His aunt is Irene Dunne, the movie actress. Charles was going to show us around Hollywood when we got back. He was an up-and-coming young actor himself. He received many letters from the topnotch artist in Hollywood. Mary Alice, I wish you could have known him, because I believe he had the greatest sense of humor I've ever known.

In the battery Saturday afternoon, we got incoming mail—41 rounds of 76 [76 mm Russian artillery shells]. There was no damage done, except our tents are full of holes. This sort of makes me mad, because I had just gotten a new tent. My boys here are dug in well.

Honey, you said you wanted to know what we have done, so that is it for now. It is not a very pretty sight and please don't say anything about what I've said outside the family. Why don't you just burn this letter?

∞⚹∞

I never heard a word about Hill 749 until I started this project. I wonder if Mom told anyone? It may have been too difficult for her to talk about it, but I am glad she didn't burn the letter as Dad suggested.

I will interrupt Dad's letter right here to tell an incredibly moving story that happened simultaneously during the battle of Hill 749. It is best told in the following medal of honor citation:

JOSEPH VITTORI

Corporal, U.S. Marine Corps Reserve
Company F, 2nd Battalion, 1st Marines
1st Marine Division (Rein.)
Hill 749, Korea
15 and 16 September 1951

CITATION

For conspicuous gallantry and intrepidity at the risk of his life above and beyond the call of duty while serving as an automatic-rifleman in Company F, in action against enemy aggressor forces. With a forward platoon suffering heavy casualties and forced to withdraw under a vicious enemy counterattack as his company assaulted strong hostile forces entrenched on Hill 749, Cpl. Vittori boldly rushed through the withdrawing troops with 2 other volunteers from his reserve platoon and plunged directly into the midst of the enemy. Overwhelming them in a fierce hand-to-hand struggle, he enabled his company to consolidate its positions to meet further imminent onslaughts. Quick to respond to an urgent call for a rifleman to defend a heavy machine gun positioned on the extreme point of the northern flank and virtually isolated from the remainder of the unit when the enemy again struck in force during the night, he assumed position under the devastating barrage. Fighting a single-handed battle, he leaped from 1 flank to the other, covering each foxhole in turn as casualties continued to mount, manning a machine gun when the gunner was struck down and making repeated trips through the heaviest shellfire to replenish ammunition. With the situation becoming extremely critical, reinforcing units to the rear pinned down under the blistering attack and foxholes left practically void by dead and wounded for a distance of 100 yards, Cpl. Vittori continued his valiant stand, refusing to give ground as the enemy penetrated to within feet of his position, simulating strength in the line and denying the foe physical occupation of the ground. Mortally wounded by the enemy machine gun and rifle bullets while persisting in his magnificent defense of the sector where approximately 200 enemy dead were found the following morning, Cpl. Vittori, by his fortitude, stouthearted courage, and great personal valor, had kept the point position intact despite the tremendous odds and undoubtedly prevented the entire battalion position from collapsing. His extraordinary heroism throughout the furious nightlong battle reflects the highest credit upon himself and the U.S. Naval Service. He gallantly gave his life for his country.[19]

⚬⚬⚬

I'm sure Dad knew of Corporal Vittori's incredible valor. This was the same night Lieutenant Laney was calling down Easy Battery's fire, and Dad lost Lieutenant Dench and his radio operator to mortar fire. It was conventional ground warfare at its utmost.

Dad never talked much about the war. He would answer questions, but he never volunteered much about his involvement or what he had seen. As a young boy, I knew he shot large artillery rounds that exploded and probably killed enemy soldiers.

I had seen that in the movies. I wanted to ask him if he had ever killed an enemy soldier with a gun, but I just couldn't do it. Until I read this letter, I had no idea he experienced the horrors of war to this extent. I cry every time I read it.

On several occasions, when I asked Dad questions about the war, he would say, "You know things are fixing to get rough when the word is passed down the line to fix bayonets." Many Marines were bayonetted to death in the Korean War. Both the North Koreans and the Chinese were experts in hand-to-hand combat and used bayonets frequently.

The following is an excerpt from John Nolan's **The Run-Up to the Punch Bowl: A Memoir of the Korean War, 1951.** *Nolan was a rifle platoon leader in Baker Company, 1st Battalion, 1st Marines. Dad's buddies in Dog Battery were supporting the 1st Battalion and Baker Company with artillery fire during the battle of Hill 749.*

It was 14:30 on the afternoon of the 16th. Hill 749 had just been strafed and bombed twice by a squadron of Navy Corsairs.

Dog Battery had pummeled the North Koreans with a final 105 Howitzer barrage. It was time for Baker Company to move out. The battle had been much tougher than they expected, and the plan for the final assault had been recently revised.

Navy F4U Corsairs

"It's a big hill, and we spread out across it—three platoons abreast, bayonets fixed. We start up. The artillery and big mortars have finished. Now the heavy machine guns are firing just in front of us and our company; 60 mm mortars are landing about 50 yards out and moving ahead as we advance. On this hill, it works. Before we get to the top, everyone is firing, moving on up the hill and over the enemy positions. We pick up a few wounded NKs [North Koreans] on the way. But otherwise we roll over the top. It may be anti-climactic, but Hill 749 is finally ours."[20]

There were many American war heroes during the three-day battle for Hill 749, and Corporal John Nolan was certainly one of them. Our nation will forever be indebted.

The following story is one Dad told me and there is a good chance it happened right after the battle for Hill 749.

Dad was back in the battery, and one of his men came driving up with a North Korean's head mounted on the front of the Jeep. Dad was incensed, and the soldier was severely reprimanded. I doubt it was to the extent of an official reprimand, but regardless of what had happened, that was not the way Dad's battery operated. As a young boy, the story spooked me a little, and I have never forgotten it.

The Navy Corsair was one of the most iconic fighters of World War II and the Korean War. With a 2,000 HP (horsepower) radial engine and a top speed of 417 miles per hour, it could out-climb, out-run, and out-fight any propeller-driven aircraft it faced. Known for its distinctive design and huge, thirteen-foot diameter, three-bladed propeller, the aircraft was also known for the peculiar sound it made at higher airspeed. It was called "Whistling Death," and you know that was a welcome sound to the Marines on Hill 749.[21]

On Christmas day around 1959, Santa Claus brought me one of my favorite presents that year, a navy-blue Corsair model airplane. Dad always loved that plane, and now I know why.

After reading this letter, I have no doubt Mom was completely beside herself. It is almost surrealistic that Dad could report this type of war news and then shift out of it in one sentence. I'm sure his letter writing was good therapy and a way of coping with what was happening in the war.

So much for the war, now we will go on with more news. I got your package with the notebooks, and listen, gal, they are exactly what I need. How in the world did you find such good ones? Thanks a lot!

I got a letter from Lila and I. E. the other day and certainly did enjoy reading it. She sure seems to like our John.

Little lady, you have certainly kept me well-informed with your letters. I got 4 in the past 2 days. I am thrilled to death about the car payments and if you would like I can mail more money to you in the near future. I sure hope you got the $200 check. What about the money from the MC [Marine Corps] on your travel home pay?

Did you get to see my brother as he passed through Greenville? I sure hope he gets into a good outfit.

Mary Alice, I'm wondering if you would do the following for me as you have time. I have an interpreter with me now by the name of YOUNG HUN. I call him Pete for short. He is a very smart boy: 23 years of age, and he speaks English quite well. He can also speak Japanese and Korean. He has asked me to inquire about exchange of students in the States. He has been very nice to me and does so much work in taking care of my personal gear that I told him I would inquire. I thought that Lila and I. E. could find out about the possibilities of scholarship in the University. He is a deserving boy and should be given a chance at higher education so that someday, in a small way, he could help raise his people out of the rut they are in.

I would like to hear John say some of his rhymes and tell me some of his stories. I'll bet they are cute.

It is sure getting cold here at night, and today I'm going to try and make some makeshift stoves for the battery. We will probably get stoves, but it will be so cold by then I doubt if we could light them. Ha Ha!

Honey bug, you be sweet and take care of our boy.

I love you, sweetheart.

Your husband,

Al XX

∝⋙⊂

I love that Dad made an effort to help his interpreter. Mom's older sister, Lila, would eventually become Dean of Women at the University of Texas at Austin, and I'm sure she already had good contacts there. I do not know if anything ever came of it.

And finally, he got his notebooks and put them to immediate use:

- S+a meeting

INTERPRETERS ASSIGNED 2-11				
NAME	CLASS	REGIMENT DATE JOINED	SECTION	
KIM HAK SONG	II	14 APR 51	'F'	450 WON
KIM YOUNG KAP	I	22 NOV 51		370 WON
CHUNG KYONG HI	I	8 DEC. 51		370 WON

2.

INTERPRETERS PAY SCALE

CLASS I	370 WON PER. HR.
CLASS II	450 WON PER HR.
CLASS III	530 WON PER HR.

General Duties of Battalion Staff Off.

To: 1. Make a continuous study of the situation.

2. Inform the commander and other staff officers concerning the situation as it pertains to their functions.

3. Advise the commander and make Recommendations Concerning their Specialties

4. Prepare Policies, Estimates, plans, and Orders or parts of Orders pertaining to their duties.

5. Maintain Required records and Others as needed to enable them to function properly.

INTELLIGENCE OFFICER (S-2)

I. Primary function is:

 A. THE LOCATION OF TARGETS ON WHICH THE BATTALION MAY FIRE.

II. OTHER DUTIES.

 A. Collects information on the
  1. ENEMY (Primarily Artillery Targets)
  2. Terrain
  3. Weather

 B. Records, Evaluates, and Interprets information Collected.

 C. Disseminates information & Intelligence

 D. Directs & Coordinates Intelligence — gathering agencies.

 E. Plans & Supervises intelligence training.

HOW TO FIND RANGE OF SOVIET 76.2 mm DIVISIONAL GUN.

x = range to piece

v = velocity of shell   308 yds per sec.

s = speed of SOUND   360 yds per sec.

t = time of Bang to explosion

f = time of sound from piece to explosion

$$\frac{x}{v} = f \qquad f - t = \frac{x}{s}$$

$$\frac{x}{v} - t = \frac{x}{s}$$

$$\frac{x}{v} - \frac{x}{s} = t$$

$$sx - vx = vst$$

$$x = \frac{vst}{s - v}$$

MONDAY 24 SEPTEMBER 1951

Dear Mary Alice and John,

Gosh, I sure have been getting a lot of mail from you lately. That is one thing that always keeps me going, and yours are always full of news. Thanks a million for so many.

The package with the five cans of nuts arrived two days ago. The nuts were delicious and we've eaten them all. They sure go well with our beer ration. We get 8 cans of beer a week. I can hardly wait until other things come. Also, that same day the package came, I got a small package from Mother and Dad that contained samples of material they are using on the house. Boy, I am making out in the mail calls! Thanks too for the goodies; they sure help out.

Just a few minutes ago I received a copy of a letter from Colonel Heely (my battalion commander) that was sent to commanding general, 1st Marine Division, FMF [Fleet Marine Force]. The letter has to do with clearance of me to handle classified material up to and including SECRET. They had an FBI man out, and he took fingerprints and also filled out many forms. He said they would check up on me in the States. So, if you have any strange callers asking about me, you'll know they are from the FBI [Federal Bureau of Investigation]. They will probably check in Greenville, Quinlan, Brownwood, Commerce and who knows where else. I just wanted you to know though.

Well, the fighting here on the front goes on and on day in and day out. We are gaining ground every day, but the price we pay is heavy. The 2nd Battalion 1st Marines are in reserve now, and we are in general support;

however, in the near future we will again be committed. The 1st and 3rd Battalions are now on the line. The other day, about 1,000 yards in front of us, a company of Marines took a hill by helicopter. This is the first time this has ever been done, but it sure worked. I expect the 2nd Battalion will try it next. You will more than likely hear about it over the radio.

These Koreans are tricky—the other day one came up to the front lines and said he wanted to surrender himself and about a battalion of men. We agreed, but when they were about 200 yards away from us, they opened fire. So, we had to clobber them. Bill Guynes and Pete Bell were the boys calling down the artillery in that operation. Bill is from Shreveport and Pete is from Dallas. So much for the war.

Honey, it was certainly nice of you to treat my brother so well at the end of his civilian career. I know he enjoyed himself very much. I'll bet the best part was playing with John.

As soon as I am paid, I will send you another check for $200. I have already asked for it, and it should come out in a week or two. From now on though, I will let it ride on the books. I will be so glad to get out of debt that I won't know what to do. Of course, there has been nothing pressing about the matter, but you know how we feel about those things. Say, did you ever get your travel pay from camp Pendleton?

Baby, I don't want you to go wanting for anything in the way of clothes. Why don't you go on a buying spree and get you a lot? I love for you to have pretty things. So, get them! Also, as we get money along, I would like to try and save a little. Maybe sometime we can build a house and get started living right. I'll save what I get here and maybe that will help out too.

You have asked me several times about when I think I will be coming home. To give a truthful answer—no one knows. But here is the scoop as it now stands. A Marine Corps bulletin out recently stated that all reserves in my class would be out of Corps by June '52. However, I expect to be out of Korea possibly by February 18, 1952. If the rotation keeps up, I could be out of Korea by December 18, 1951. Now don't get your hopes up for the latter, because it is too early to determine. Here are the dates I have to work on: (1) Started active duty March 18, 1951. (2) Left U.S. June 18, 1951. (3) Arrived to Korea July 6, 1951. They are letting guys go home on regimental level. If I can get a list, I'll let you know where I stand, and we may be able to determine something from that. I'll close now until next time.

—Until then—

I love you,

Al, XX

∝≫○

Dad did receive his "SECRET" clearance.

It sounds like Mom had been inquiring for some time about when Dad would be coming home. For the first time, Dad cautioned her, but also said it was possible he could be out of Korea by as early as December 18th. As I said, Dad was an optimist.

∝≫○

29 SEPTEMBER 1951

Dear Mary Alice,

It is raining today and it is turning quite cold. In our present position though, we do not have to worry much about the weather. We all have large pyramidal tents up and things are quite dry. For the time being we have stopped our attack and are digging in to defend what ground we have taken. About the main reason we have stopped is that we don't have the manpower to keep on going. When more replacements come in, we will go on, but for now we are set. I'll tell you a little bit about our present position, so you can get some idea as to how we are set up.

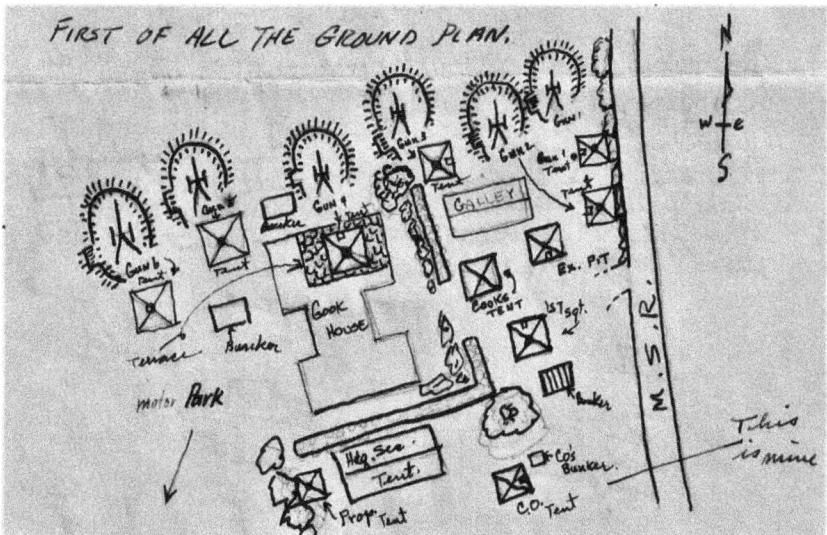

The ground plan is very crowded as I have drawn it, but really, we are spread out. However, it does show how we are now set up. I'll draw some more to explain further.

⬦⬦⬦

When I was young and asked Dad a question, he often told me to "go get a piece of paper and a pencil and I'll show you." He loved to sketch almost anything and was very good at maps or top views that showed how things were oriented. He typically included a compass showing the orientation of the drawing. He sketched a variety of compasses from simple (as pictured on page 105) to elaborate on a more formal drawing. I practiced very hard trying to duplicate Dad's compasses and I use them to this day on simple drawings that I occasionally make.

⬦⬦⬦

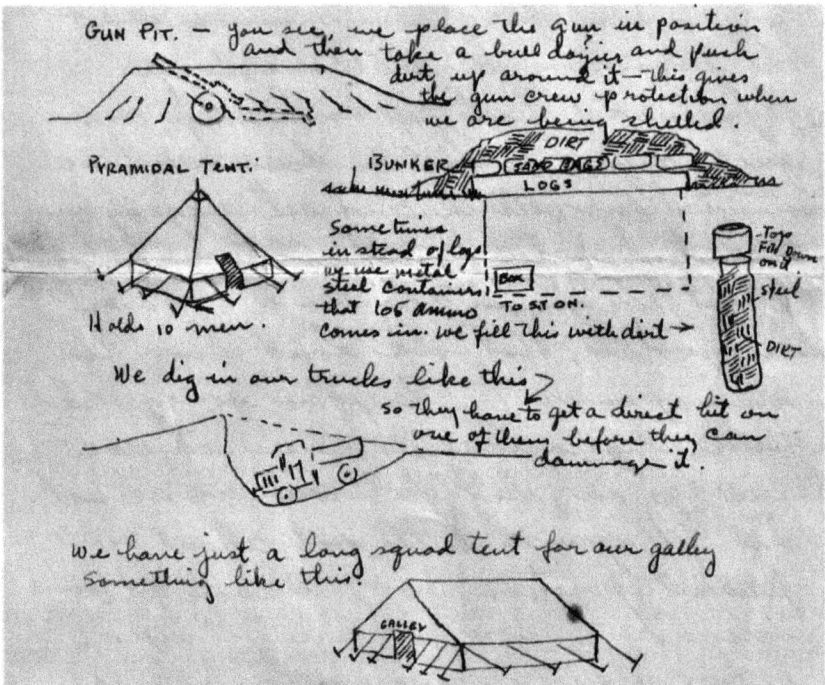

This will give you some idea as to what our setup is. Perhaps before long I can send you some real pictures of our battery. Yesterday, we got in our mountain sleeping bags. They are sure warm too and built like a comforter with feathers on the inside. I sleep very warm at night. Two days ago, I also made a stove for my tent. It's like this.

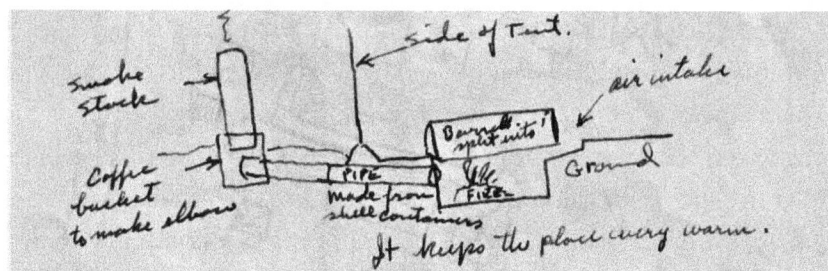

Mary Alice, you also ask about how we sleep. Things are more or less secure now, and we just have post (local security) on watch at all hours. However, when things are rough, you have little time for sleep. The longest I've been awake at one stretch so far is 2 nights and 3 days. I always sleep with my S & W, and we don't sleep too hard either. The weather can get cold around here (so we are told), and I'm sure that it's true. The Marine Corps will provide us with clothing that should keep us warm—long underwear, wool shirts, alpaca lined vest and hats, also coats, boots, gloves, etc. We haven't gotten all the clothes as yet, but we have enough for now and the others will come. I got a letter from Mother yesterday saying she had sent Aunt Alice some money to buy me a hand warmer. You know, like the one Dad has. Well, I got two warmers from Aunt Alice plus a little red metal box they were mailed in. Boy, I'll keep good and warm now, and I can sure use the box too.

Uncle Les has sent me a subscription to TIME MAGAZINE. Baby, this is one thing that will be welcome, because we have a hard time trying to keep up with the news. If you see him, tell him thanks and I will write soon. You see, I am fixed up very well.

Honey, this is a little ahead of time but I think I'll let you know what I plan to do. For Christmas, I'm going to try and buy us a Revier 8 mm motion picture camera and a projector. I have written the PX in Yokohama and asked them to write me about the total cost on the camera and projector. If I can swing this deal, you will receive a projector and I'll keep the camera. All we would have to do then is keep film going back-and-forth. I'm sure you would get a kick out of it. I know I would. The film would be something we would always be proud of. So, don't be surprised if one of these days you get a Revier 8 mm projector. And then, you will get a little later some film to send off and have developed. Then you can see how your husband is doing. (I said this before but don't look now for the $200 check coming—I believe I'll go through with it now.) I'll stop for now and continue later.

It is now the morning of October 2.

Honey, I have had many administrative details to attend to since I last started writing. I've had to write up two letters of commendation and one Bronze Star. These are for the boys in the battery. They put out a fire on an ammo truck that was started when we were being shelled. Some of the fragments hit the truck and set it off. In our forward observation teams, we have three letters of commendation and three bronze stars also. The boys sure deserve them.

Mary Alice, I got a letter from you yesterday telling me about your trip to Dallas and what you got, including the non-mated shoes. Ha! You will make it work out OK I know. You also said you wanted to know about me. Well, other than what I've already said, we generally get for breakfast two eggs, three hotcakes with jelly, bacon, coffee and breakfast cereal. Sometimes we have gravy on toast. I miss the fresh milk mostly. Dinner and supper, we generally have meat, two vegetables with bread, and fruit drink. Sometimes we have cake, and about every two weeks we get some ice cream. I have been doing very well on the food but I have lost a lot of weight. I think it is very becoming to me though. I'm getting that old "Gung Ho" spirit again! The pants I brought over with me just hang. I have so many duties that it almost seems impossible to put them down on paper. But first of all, I am responsible for the firing of my six Howitzers in the close and continuous support of the infantry. I have to take care of all my boys at all times. Keep the trucks running and chow coming through, write reports, and many other things. Right now, I'm going to make out a chart on men in my battery who would like to go to college on the NROTC [Naval Reserve Officers Training Corps] program. It looks like we will have about 15. Next week I will start cold-weather school. I'm going to call it "COLD FACTS FOR KEEPING WARM." I hope it works this winter. Mary Alice, I have found the name of the company that makes the stencil marking pencils.

"MARKTEX – Resist Ink"
"Launder-proof Permanent Cloth Marking"

MFD BY: MARK-TEX CORP
453 W 17TH ST
NEW YORK, NY

I just happened to take this down when I saw one the other day. Also, on my want list is a roll of scotch tape and red, green, blue and black grease marking pencils—also a ruler. These things are hard to get out here, but they sure come in handy. Also, you might send some flashlight bulbs extra for my flashlight you are sending.

Today is Wednesday, October 3, 1951.

Mary Alice, I just haven't had time to finish writing so string along with me. I just got four letters from you yesterday, two of them contain letters from Offie. It's the funniest thing about Offie's letters in that they were funny and very cleverly written, but what's more is my experience with trying to read them. When I first opened them up and sat down to read, old Pistol Pete over the hill opened up with four rounds. I didn't get to read a word, but I hit my hole fast. Well, that's all that came in that time. So, I got out of my hole and started to read again and got through the first sentence and BANG, here they come again. Back in the hole again. I waited about 3 minutes and tried to read again—and the same thing happened again. It just seemed the Gooks didn't want me to read Offie's letter. OK, I let them have their way for about an hour with no rounds in the area. So, I take them out again and start to read this time and only two sentences down, what do you know, 2 rounds in! Truly I can't believe Offie's letters had anything to do with the shooting, but everything pointed in that direction. I read them this morning with a sharp eye out, and nothing happened. Just a lot of fun anyway! Thanks so much for sending them. I can just see him with his icebox (THE THING)—electric?

One of my boys got a Silver Star yesterday when one of the incoming rounds hit the 1st Marine ammo dump. He took over our CAT and put the fire out at great risk to his own personal safety. We were sure proud of him, because he more than likely saved many lives had that thing exploded all the way.

Do you remember Madison? He was with the 3rd Battalion 11th Marines. He phoned me about two weeks ago and asked me to come and see him when I had time. Well, I passed by his outfit a few days ago, and I dropped in only to find out he had stepped on a landmine and was in the Tokyo General Hospital. They said his condition was serious. I expect he will be all right, though.

Mama, keep the letters coming and telling me about our boy. He sure must be getting to be a corker. I like that about wanting to know my name. Please don't let him forget me, and, Mama, you had better start thinking about our boy's Christmas. You'll need lots of things. This is sure a messy letter. I'll try to do better next time.

I love you.

Love from your husband,

Al

∝⋙∽

What an incredible, information-packed letter spanning six days. I love Dad's drawings that give a firsthand account of how Easy Battery was actually laid out. And, he was sure pitching Mom hard to get that movie camera!

Dad also needed scotch tape, colored grease-marking pencils, and a ruler. I'm surprised he didn't have those items. I believe one of his important responsibilities was updating the clear overlays for the battle maps, which showed the changes taking place in the field. The maps would have been presented to his superior officers in planning meetings. Dad was a stickler for accuracy, but he also wanted the overlays to be easily understood and look professional.

Dad said he was going to make a chart of the fifteen men he had who wanted to take advantage of the NROTC program. In the midst of an all-out war, I doubt if that was a requirement sent down from division headquarters (although I may be wrong on this). I believe that was Dad just staying organized and looking after his troops, just like he tried to help his interpreter in a previous letter.

And as long as you are going to teach a cold weather school, why not give it a creative name like COLD FACTS FOR KEEPING WARM? That was definitely Dad's style.

⟨⟩

OCTOBER 6, 1951

Dear Mary Alice and John,

Honey, your husband is doing fine. We work hard here and there always seem to be plenty more jobs ahead. To me, time is short because a day just doesn't have enough hours in it to do all the jobs I would like to do. We keep plugging along, and maybe someday it will come to an end.

I had a compliment paid to me today that I guess I'll never forget. It was like this. About 10 o'clock this morning, during a fire mission in which we had all six of our guns blazing away, a jeep drove up with guys in them carrying movie cameras, tape recorders, etc. Well, they got out and I went over and inquired about what they wanted. They wanted to make pictures of my battery in action. Well, I knew it would do the kids good to have themselves on film so I let them start. These fellows were from division. Anyway, after the pictures were taken, they asked us all to group around and be interviewed. The question came up as to who was to be interviewed and all my boys said they wanted their Skipper to speak for them. You see, they call me their Skipper. I made the interview which was mostly about the fighting here, but right at the last, they asked me if I had anything I wanted to say to you. Well, honey, I kind of got all choked up and didn't say the things I would like to have said to you because there were just too many people standing around. I hope you understand. Now this recording was to be sent to Dallas sometime and after they get through using it, it will be given to you. So, you can hear what your husband had to say.

Today I received mail from your dad and mother, Uncle Harvey, my mother and you. I just don't know what to say about so many letters, but tell each and every one of them I deeply appreciate their thoughtfulness and I thank them from the bottom of my heart.

Baby, I'm enclosing a piece of paper that contains the address of John Adams and his wife. I saw him yesterday, and he gave it to me. He said for you to write her and ask her for the snapshots of us. He said they were all fairly good. In writing, you might enclose money for them. She is also PG [pregnant], and John is just as happy as he can be about it. Tell her that he's looking fine and doing a damn good job. He is FO'ing for the KMC.

I haven't written my Dad yet. You know October 4 is his birthday. So, I propose to do that now. Thanks again for everything. Our boy John must be cute. Every letter I get I just read over and over again the part telling about the cute things he does. Mama Bess sure told some good ones on him.

Be sweet.

I love *you,*

Al

✂✂

I don't know if anything ever came of the film or the tape-recorded interview.

Chapter 9
KANSONG

19 OCTOBER 1951

Dear Mary Alice and John,

Well, your old man has been very poor on his writing for some time now, but it is not entirely my fault. You see, we are still in the same position that we have been in since about September 10, and there always seems to be something coming up to keep me busy. However, the fact that I haven't written is water under the bridge, and I'll try to make up for it starting right now.

First of all, I'll locate myself on your map. Lieutenant Steele, my assistant executive officer, has a map like ours. He and his wife have a similar system as ours started out to be, however I fouled the deal up. If you will look in the square 38°-128°, you will see the town of KANSONG on the coast of the Sea of Japan. It looks something like this:

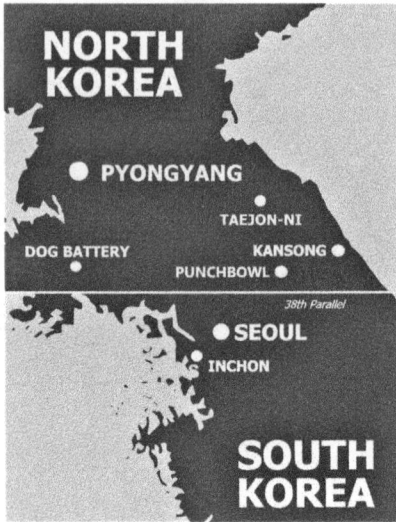

It is hard to locate yourself accurately on such a small-scale map as this, but it is approximately correct. Our front lines are along the little triangles E-1, E-2, E-3. My forward observer teams and the battery are just off to the left of the trail (which is now a two-lane road), as shown. From E-3 position, you can see down the river all the way to HONGSONG and the sea. The front lines are now about 3 miles in front of the battery.

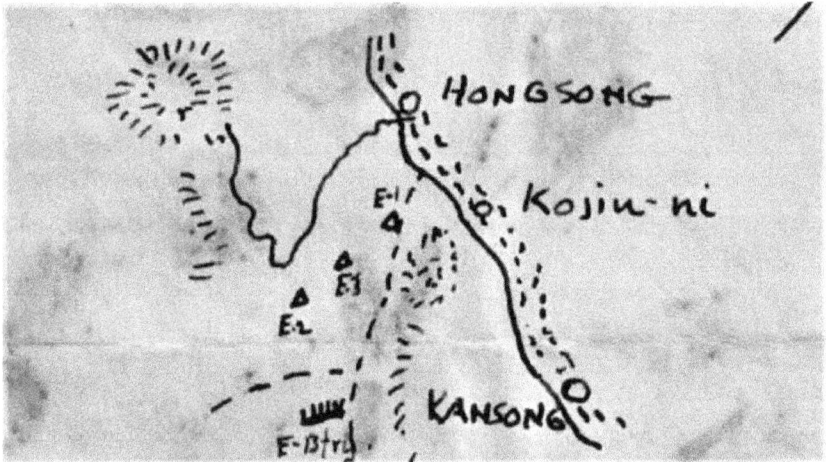

Location of KANSONG

I go up to visit my FO about once a week. I take supplies up and try to make them feel they are still a part of the battery, even though they stay with the infantry. It's a long hard walk over these hills to get up there. I had an experience that I don't want to have again for a long time the last time I went up to see them. I stayed up nearly all day shooting the breeze with Colonel Ryehart, the 1st Marine's CO [commanding officer], walking the lines and discussing the best areas to cover with artillery in case of an attack. Well, anyway I left the hill about 5 PM with a couple of my boys that I always take with me for protection. You see, it's always better to go at least in twos because we have many snipers behind our lines and they are rather reluctant to fire at a group because one of us would get them for sure. We started down and a very heavy fog set in from the sea and it was becoming dark also. I was unable to locate myself on the map because I couldn't see the outstanding terrain features around me. I had a compass and could have followed it and it would have led me out, but this area is heavily mined so I didn't want to take off through the boondocks. So, we picked out a nice bunker that the Gooks abandoned and spent the night. We had no trouble throughout the night but we nearly froze. However, the next morning we made it in OK. The people around here were very worried about us and we were reported MIA [missing in action] for that. I hope it didn't go any further than the division command post. I'll never do that again.

We can't tell how true it is, because tomorrow we may move out, but for now we are digging in for the winter. My tent has a wooden deck, a GI [government issue] stove, plus a beautiful bright red parachute that I picked up from an air drop. I have built a desk, a stool, and a light fixture—also an in and out box for the desk. This is taking up most of my time. Our winter gear is now arriving in large quantities, and we have to show the boys how to wear each garment.

Mary Alice, you are the sweetest girl to write me so often that I don't believe I could get along without your letters. I heard from Aunt Mary Earle yesterday and along with the letter, she had some pictures that they had taken when last at Jefferson. I sure do enjoy looking at them.

In your last four or five letters you have mentioned that you hope I get a better job. I'm sorry if I gave you that impression when talking about being investigated to have classified material. You see, as I am now, many times I have to carry documents that are top-secret. Plans of attack, etc. That is all that is for.

Honey, I am so proud of you for the fact that you have paid off the debt on our car and still have money in the bank. To add to it, you should be getting another check from my insurance one of these days. I also have a check in my billfold for $200 that I may send home soon if I can't buy the camera I have wanted so long. Tell me what you think of this idea.

Baby, I miss you so much it hurts most of the time. If you were only here things would be much easier. When I get back, little lady, you had better stand by for another honeymoon. I can hardly wait to see our boy. I'll bet he has grown so much. He must have—chewing gum and carrying groceries in from the store.

Remember I love you only, and take care of our boy.

Your husband,

Al

Dad sure seems nonchalant about walking with two of his men through the hills (with snipers in the area) to go and visit his forward observers. Mom definitely did not like his experience, which resulted in being reported MIA. To survive a war, sometimes luck needs to be on your side.

Also, don't you love Dad's tent? He had it all fixed up with a deck, stove, desk, light fixture, stool, and an in/out box. I'm sure the red parachute was tastefully displayed. This was his office, and I guarantee you he had a place for all the graphic arts tools he was collecting from Mom.

And once again, Dad pitches Mom on the movie camera idea. He even goes to the extent of revealing a $200 check he can pay for it with (or send home if she nixes the idea). Obviously, she has not commented on it in her return letters. The movie camera purchase just wasn't making Mom's priority list with her husband in the midst of an all-out war.

∞⧓∞

SUNDAY OCTOBER 21, 1951

My Dear Mary Alice and John

All day today I have been waiting for the regimental commander, Colonel Burton, to come by and visit my battery. It has been cold and rainy, so I guess the weather was too much for him. Anyway, he hasn't shown up. Had he come through, we would have been ready, because I've had the boys out really cleaning the place up. His main objective in coming I believe was to see how our guns are dug in and to introduce his executive officer to everyone. In time, he will become our new battalion commander. Colonel Heely's time is just about up, and I expect by the first he will be relieved.

If I remember right, today I've been in Korea three months and 15 days and in three more days I will have been out of the States for 1/3 of a year. To write it down doesn't sound so very long, but it has been a very long time. When I get back, I hope this will never happen again. In your last letter, you also sent along a clipping from the Dallas paper. Baby, what that boy was writing is true facts. I know, because that just happened up in front of us. I don't believe I am as shaky about anything as I am the land mines. You lose a foot or a leg once you step on one. We lost a truck about two weeks ago that ran over one in the road. The driver got hit in the legs but not hurt so very bad. The front of the truck was blown off.

Enclosed you will find a price list of merchandise that the Japan Central Exchange has to offer now. It would be rather hard to buy something without being able to see them or get a better description; however, I do know they handle very high-class goods. I thought perhaps you might see something here you would like to have either for yourself or to give as gifts for Christmas. Anyway, I thought you would get a kick out of it.

HEADQUARTERS
JAPAN CENTRAL EXCHANGE
APO 503

CHRISTMAS MERCHANDISE

The merchandise listed below includes the leading brands from the Far East and the United States of America. Only merchandise from well known manufacturers is listed. Weights listed are figured to the nearest pound.

	WT.			WT.	
LEATHER GOODS			WOMENS WEAR		
Billfolds and Wallets	1	$2.50- 5.00	Night Gowns	1	$2.00- 8.50
Gadget Bags	2	8.00- 12.00	Hosiery	1	1.10
Mens Fitted Cases	3	5.30- 21.00	Panties, 7/Box	2	2.50
			Robes	2	4.00-12.00
LUGGAGE			Scarves	1	.50- 2.65
Fortnighter Case	8	25.00- 40.00	Slips	1	1.60- 7.00
Overnight Case	4	15.00- 40.00	Slippers	1	1.50- 6.70
Two Suiters	8	22.00- 40.00	Sweaters	1	2.00-10.00
Vanity Cases	4	15.00- 25.00	Blouses	1	5.00- 8.00
Wardrobe Cases	8	25.00- 40.00	Gloves	1	1.00- 4.00
			Slipper Socks	1	2.50
CAMERAS AND ACCESSORIES					
Movie, 8 and 16mm	6	44.85-199.00	Photo Albums	1	1.75- 2.20
Still	3	4.10- 59.00	Playing Cards, Plastic	1	4.10- 6.00
Exposure Meters	1	19.45- 21.70	Desk Sets	2	7.75-21.20
Radios, Portable or Table Models-Max.75#			Fountain Pens	1	1.10-10.60
		19.45- 87.90	Pen and Pencil Sets	1	2.65-19.00
Record Players	6	23.60	Mechanical Pencils	1	.60- 3.05
Handee Kit	2	20.05	Boxed Stationery	1	.75- 3.15
Typewriters, Portable	20	49.00- 69.95	Cigars, Box	4	2.50- 6.00

Sample of Christmas items at the PX in Japan

I got a very nice letter from Offie yesterday. It sure sounds as though he has a good class schedule. Wish that I had one like that. Maybe next year I can.

I just got a call from our battalion S-2 (intelligence), and it seems that the ROKs [Republic of Korea (South Korea)] on our right flank have let a battalion of Gooks get through their lines. They are circling back around to try and knock out some of our artillery. Excuse me while I have our local security break out their hand grenades and throw a round into the chamber of their machine guns."

OK, that's done. If they come this way, we will have a hot welcome for them.

You will laugh when you read this—your husband now has a mustache. Ha Ha! It's black and long and twists to two fine points on the end. You would really burst your sides laughing if you could see me.

In all of your letters you mentioned many of the things that our baby boy has been doing. He sure sounds like a real little man. Keep me posted on all that he does, because I just live on things like that. I could just see him in his little jammies with the feet, asleep, all nice and clean. I'll bet he can really get dirty sometimes though. If you have time, why don't you snap some pictures and send me some of you both.

Baby, I had better stop now and try and get a little sleep.

Love you so much,

XX Al

On more than one occasion in his letters, Dad stops writing to deal with the war. Here, the enemy was circling around to try and knock out his Howitzers. He alerted his men, and they prepared to give the enemy a "hot welcome" if they tried anything. Dad then appeared to calmly resume writing his letter. I wonder if war ever becomes matter-of-fact? After a while, I think it must.

Dad mentions ordering his local security guards to "throw a round into the chamber of their machine guns." On more than one occasion, Dad talked to me about the Browning Automatic Rifle (BAR). He simply referred to it as a "BAR" and I suspect that was what his local security guards were using. I simply remember that Dad had a huge amount of respect for the BAR and its firepower.

The BAR was designed in 1917 by John Browning and remained in production until 1945. It fired a .30-06 Springfield cartridge at a rate of 550 rounds/min. and had a standard 20-round detachable magazine. With an effective firing range of up to 1500 yards, the BAR was designed to be carried by each designated soldier on a shoulder strap and fired from the hip. However, it was usually used as a light machine gun and fired from a bi-pod. [There were approximately 9 BARs in a Marine infantry platoon.][22]

The BAR was essential in helping U.S. and UN forces break up the massed "human wave" infantry charges by Chinese and North Korean troops during the Korean War. It was one of the few automatic firearms in the Allied inventory capable of functioning in the harsh winter combat conditions on brutal Korean battlefields. The BAR was a highly respected weapon in the Marine Corps.[23]

M1918 Browning Automatic Rifle (BAR),
.30 caliber, 20-shot magazine

NOVEMBER 5, 1951

My Dear Mary Alice and John,

Honey, your last letter was sure welcome, because you keep me so
well posted on the news around home. I should be kicked for not
writing more than I do, but time does pass fast and I keep so busy
that sometimes more passes than I realize. A day still doesn't seem to
contain enough hours, for so many things have to be done. Tell John
that I certainly did enjoy his letter. That boy will be so big and grown
by the time I see him, that I won't recognize him.

We have been having a little trouble with incoming mail here recently. Dog Battery, the other day lost 1 man (KIA) and 4 (WIA). Also
lost two 105 Howitzers, five (6 x 6) trucks, tents, stoves, etc. Easy
[Battery] has been lucky because I haven't lost a thing yet. Please
don't say anything in public about our losses, because we are not supposed to mention them at all. Everything else is normal, and we are
still in the same position. I don't know whether or not I mentioned

it, but the package with the flashlight and Lance cookies came in and were in excellent condition. Thanks ever so much for everything. The boys really went for the Lance products, and any more that will be forthcoming will be welcome.

Today we sent the last of the Inchon men home, and I was never so glad in all my life to see anyone go so much as I was them. You know, every time we send someone home, my time is drawing closer. Maybe in a few weeks I can give you more dope on when that will be. The cease fire talks sound encouraging, and perhaps they will come through. If they go through, I expect that the 1st Marine Division will be pulled out and sent somewhere else. The scuttlebutt is that we might go to Australia, or ½ to Hawaii and the rest to Camp Pendleton. Both of these ideas sound good to me, but of course it just depends.

I'm sure sorry you didn't get to make the trip to Jefferson, because I know Mother and Dad would sure like to see you. Perhaps by the time you get this letter you will have gone. Dad must sure be going on the house now that he has no other outside activities.

We have had snow here, and it is very cold. I think tonight we will probably get some. It is sort of misting out now. The Lance paper you sent me was very cute. And that reminds me of a cute paper I saw the other day. If I get a copy, I'll send you one. It is what a Marine should do upon returning to the States and how to adjust himself. It brings to light so many things we see every day that are common place to us, but to you would make your sides burst.

Bill Guynes, one of my friends from Shreveport, has asked me to paint a picture for him sometime. When it is done, I'll mail it to you.

He is the commercial artist I have told you about. In about 15 days, he will be leaving for the States because his time is up in the Corps. He will stop by and see you on his way to Louisiana. I think you'll like him. When I get back, we plan a big reunion at his house in Shreveport. He has a honey of a place out from there.

Well, baby, I must close now and write my folks. I haven't written in about a month.

I love you darling and long for the day I see you again.

XX

Al

∞✕✕∞

When Dad referred to "incoming mail," he was again talking about incoming 76 mm Russian artillery shells fired by the North Koreans.

∞✕✕∞

NOV. 7, 1951

Dear Mary Alice and John,

Honey, you will find along with this letter two pictures that one of my boys snapped this afternoon. He has one of those new kinds of cameras that develop the pictures in about two minutes. I don't know how long they will last, but they turned out pretty good. The one with me by the 105 makes me look pretty sad. Looks like I've been hit in the face with a baseball bat, but really, I still look the same. The dark picture has some scratches that I got there from carrying them around in my pocket. Hope you like them anyway.

Today I got a letter from Aunt Alice that contained three nice plastic bags. Really, I like them very much, but I don't know what in the hell I'm going to do with them. I'll find some use I'm sure.

I got a letter also a few days ago from Grandmother Rhea. It was certainly nice of her to write, and thank her for me please.

Today I had the regimental chaplain spend the day with me and he sure seemed to be a nice fellow. He came at an appropriate time, because I could offer him fresh killed grouse. I went out yesterday and shot three. Man, they were good! They are something like the quail or doves that I used to "ketch."

You sweet little lady, this is just a short note to let you know everything is going along OK. Love from your husband,

Al

GOONEY BIRD

15TH NOV. 1951

Dear Mary Alice and John,

I can just see our John working a crossword puzzle! I'll bet it is a riot. I can't imagine him doing the things you were always telling me he does. Maybe before long I'll be with you to enjoy our son.

Your letter, Mary Alice, that you did not seal, arrived yesterday just as you mailed it. I wondered who had been tampering with my mail. I posted the clipping from the Dallas News on the bulletin board and the whole battery got quite a charge from it. Mary A., I can hardly wait until my Christmas packages arrive. Have no fear about them arriving in excellent shape if they are wrapped in the same fashion as your previous ones, because they have been perfect. I don't guess I'll be mailing any packages home this year, because I don't have access to merchandise. I'll make up for it in the future though.

I'm enclosing another picture that one of my boys gave me the other day. This was taken on E-1's observation post, the morning before the night I spent on the hill. He snapped this picture while we were not looking. Lieutenant Chandler is pointing out to me several enemy strong points. I am studying the map of the area. You can tell how foggy it was in spots by the darkness of the picture. Every once in a while, we could see some movement out front. Also thought you might find the propaganda leaflets interesting.

The past few days I've been pulling a big deal to get my FOs off the hill by helicopter. I got six from the division air officer and brought them down yesterday. You have never in your life seen such happy boys as they climbed off the helicopters. This really sold them, because to walk down would have taken half a day and they made it in 8 minutes. Boy, what a deal! The way I got the idea was by taking a ride up myself a few days before. I happened to be down by "WASP" strip, and they had a helicopter going up so I just went along. I was so impressed, I decided to try and get them a ride down. It worked, so everybody is sure happy.

Today Bill Denis stopped by to say goodbye on his way to the States. He will fly out tomorrow and be on his way. He took your address and said that he and his wife would drop by and say hello on their way to Shreveport.

I now have all my boys back in the battery and we are all one big happy bunch. However, I don't know how long we will be together because there should be some big changes real soon. We are losing a lot of officers and are not getting many in. So, we may all have new jobs.

Baby, I had better close for now and join in a penny ante poker game that is going hot and heavy. Take care of our family and know I love you as always.

Love,

Al

XX

PS, I rather doubt that Edward McCollom will be right.

XX

Propaganda leaflet (front)

Propaganda leaflet (back)

Propaganda leaflet

✖

During the Korean War, one of the primary means of influencing North Korean troops and civilians was the production of propaganda leaflets. They ranged in size from 3 x 5 inches to the size of a newspaper and were delivered most often by aircraft in a special bomb with a hinged side that blew off after a predetermined amount of time. Billions of leaflets were dispensed during the war.[24]

The first leaflets (front and back) were a direct appeal to surrender and you would be treated as an honorable prisoner of war. On the second leaflet, you don't have to brush up much on your Korean to understand the message.

The Women Airforce Service Pilots (WASP) was a civilian women pilots' organization founded in September of 1942. Members of WASP became trained pilots who tested aircraft, ferried aircraft, and trained other pilots. Their purpose was to free male pilots for combat roles during World War II. The WASP program was ended on December 20, 1944. During the war, female pilots delivered over 12,000 aircraft from the factory to airbases around the world.[25]

The WASP program was not in effect during the Korean War, but Dad's reference to being down by the "WASP" strip was probably his way of communicating that the airstrip was where new planes were being ferried in for the war effort. I'm sure Mom was very proud of the efforts of the WASPs during WWII.

Chapter 10
THANKSGIVING

NOV. 24, 1951

Dear Mary Alice and John,

I haven't received a letter from you in several days and I expect it is because I have neglected writing you. I don't know why it is, but I seem to never have time to sit down and write.

We have been doing the usual of keeping the Gooks at bay. On the Marine Corps' birthday, we had quite a day blasting them since they didn't accept our invitations to the party! This all took place right at 12 noon on 10 November, and immediately afterwards we had our party. The party consisted of a formation at which I read the glories of the Corps since 1776, and then I called the youngest member and the oldest member from the battery. When they were front and center, I presented the oldest member with a sword (taken from the palace at Seoul) to cut the birthday cake (that was also front and center) and present it to the youngest member. This went off rather snappy and all enjoyed it.

My battery had the honor of entertaining the battalion executive officer for noon chow. The morning before the chow, the motions we went through were some you and I have done many times. I rather enjoyed them though. Tom Stelle (my XO) and I got a broom and swept the tent out, squared all the gear away, broke out some clean towels, and made a tablecloth for our table. We made some candelabras out of old shell casings and really spruced the place up. We had our knives, forks, and spoons laid out on the table with the mess gear in the galley. Our Korean (Lee) served the trays. It turned out very well.

Our Thanksgiving dinner also was excellent. There was so much food I could hardly stand it. Someone down the line did some good planning to have this come through. You will find a menu enclosed.

MA, the Bible you bought for yourself sounds wonderful and I will consider it a great privilege to give it to you for your birthday. May we spend many wonderful hours reading it. Happy birthday, honey. I also have another present for you. Bill Guynes sketched a picture of me and I will send it to you. It is charcoal so be careful with it.

Honey, in a few weeks I will be relieved of my battery and will go back to battalion as the S-2 (intelligence officer). All persons in this battalion are rotated in jobs after having it for four months. I'll certainly hate to leave my boys but it is just the way things go.

Before I leave, I'll get to do something I want to do. I'll get to make 12 boys sergeants and 8 corporals. I'll be very proud of accomplishing this.

Honey, I'll write again soon. Remember I love you. I'll see you and our boy someday—I hope soon.

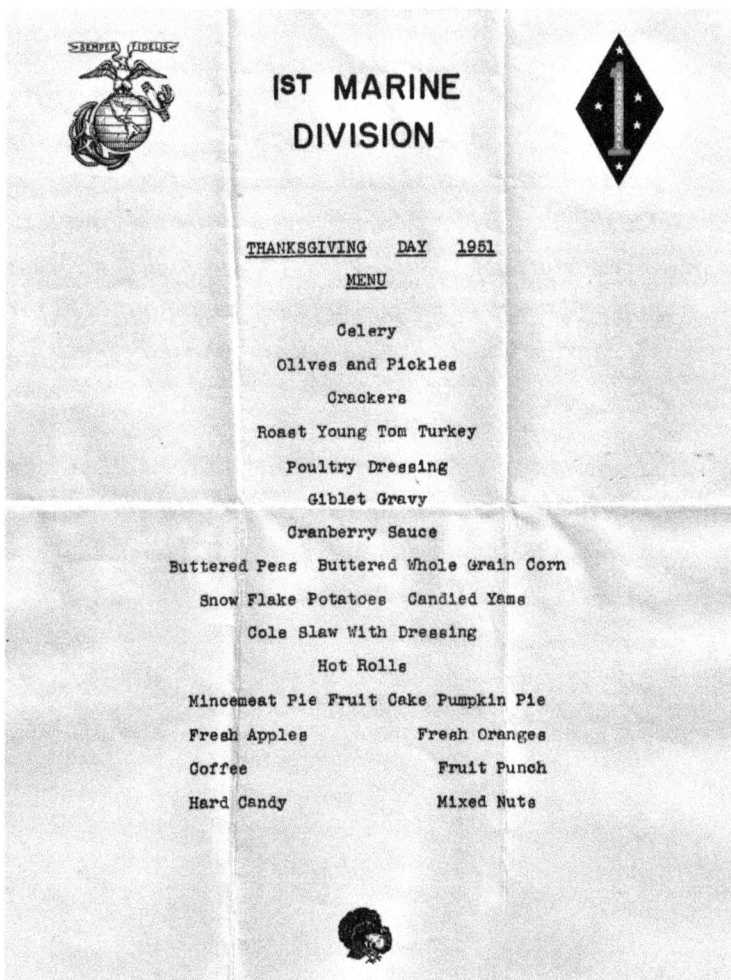

1ST MARINE DIVISION

THANKSGIVING   DAY   1951
MENU

Celery

Olives and Pickles

Crackers

Roast Young Tom Turkey

Poultry Dressing

Giblet Gravy

Cranberry Sauce

Buttered Peas   Buttered Whole Grain Corn

Snow Flake Potatoes   Candied Yams

Cole Slaw With Dressing

Hot Rolls

Mincemeat Pie Fruit Cake Pumpkin Pie

Fresh Apples   Fresh Oranges

Coffee   Fruit Punch

Hard Candy   Mixed Nuts

Love,

Al

XX – MA
XX - John

⋈

Formal celebration of the annual Marine Corps birthday begin in 1921. During the cake cutting ceremony, the first of the three pieces is presented to the guest of honor, the second to the oldest living Marine present, and the third to the youngest Marine present—a perfect way to display brotherhood and connection. This tradition is maintained as part of the Marine Corps birthday celebration on the battlefield if possible.[26]

Dad also alerted Mom that his days in the battery were coming to an end. I'm sure she was ecstatic! The winds of war seemed to be changing in her favor.

27 NOVEMBER 1951
0450

Dear Mary Alice and John,

Here I am, firing (off a letter) from the executive officer's pit this morning and, lady, it is cold. There are three of us here, and we are huddled up around the stove but good. Yesterday morning we had a little snow in the mountaintops with the valleys well covered with frost and ice. I haven't noticed any difference in this weather here than that we have around home, except it gets colder much earlier in the year. We won't mind the cold much though; it just makes it a little harder to get around.

As you can see from this paper, I got my package with it and the pencils, flashlight bulbs, Esquire calendar, rulers, scotch tape, etc. It arrived in very good condition and at record-breaking speed, but I haven't received the one containing the flashlight as yet. I am imagining you sent it by slow boat though. Tell your Dad that I certainly do enjoy carrying the little folding ruler he has sent and is something I need very often. Mary Alice, you little gal, you sure did send some good pictures of American cuties when you sent the Varga calendar. I agree with most of your comments below them, but most of them look very good. I can see you in all of them. The peanuts were good, in fact so good three of us sat down and finished them off in about 20 minutes after we got them. Mary Alice, one of the bulbs for the flashlight was bad when I tried them in a light here. Seems like the butt of one was broken. However, these will do for some time and will let you know when I need more. Thanks again for everything. In some letter you send, would you please send me my plotting needles and pens. They are light and won't take up much space. Also, if it won't be too much trouble, I would like to have the graphic site table (slide rule) for a 105 Howitzer. You can determine which one it is by looking to see if it is marked "GST 105 HOW." It can be further identified by the C & D scale having a tick mark for meters (M).

It seems like here recently every time I write home, I want you to send me something. I hope I'm not causing you too much trouble. Honey, we haven't moved at all yet and it looks as if we will stay right here in this spot for the winter. I hope I'm right about this, because it must be awful trying to move during extreme cold.

⌘

Dad continued his requests for more graphic arts materials, but I am really surprised that he had to ask for the slide rule. Dad was great with any slide rule, and this one was one specifically designed for the 105 Howitzer. I am sure he probably used it during artillery training. Why the heck didn't he already have one as a standard field issue for artillery officers in the midst of fighting a war?

⌘

SUNDAY – 2050

Baby, I started this letter some time ago, and I'm just now having time to finish it. I went back up on the hill the other day and did some shooting with my FOs. Seems we are having a lot of dispersion in our rounds. I believe now we have it fairly well squared away. This afternoon, I had my water trailer break an axle and lose a wheel. I had to get my boys with the CAT and haul it up to the battery on the blade. Things are always happening around here to keep me busy.

The peace talks sound as if some progress can be made, but it will hurt to move back and give up this ground we have fought so hard for. You can see on the map that we are the furthestmost unit in North Korea. Anyway, if it can be settled, we will gladly move back.

As each month rolls around, we see more new fellows come and old ones go. Someday, maybe I'll be boarding a ship for the U.S. As it looks now, it'll be April or May though.

I heard a story about a fella going home that I thought rather cute. It seems as though he had written his wife and said, "Honey, if you want to be the first, you better meet me at the docks." Then she, just to get back at him, wrote back, "Honey, if you want to be the next, you better catch a plane home fast." Ha! Sugar, you have very coyly neglected saying anything about my buying a movie camera. One would think you didn't approve of the idea. Answer requested!

Another thing I would like an answer on is what would you like for your birthday and Christmas. It will have to be on my list (you have). Also, what do you plan for John's Christmas? I want it to be tops.

Baby, I'll close for now so be sweet.

Love,

Al

⟶⟨⟩⟶

At first, I was confused about Dad doing "some shooting with my FOs." But then it dawned on me: this was 1951 so there were no satellites, laser range finders or GPS (Global Positioning System). All you had to go on were your maps and input from your FOs. If the map data were off, your artillery shooting was off. Dad was down there with an optical surveyor's transit, "shooting" the enemy's terrain to update his maps. He didn't like that his artillery rounds were being dispersed, and he was going to correct the situation.

And Dad's quest to get permission to buy a movie camera continued...

⟶⟨⟩⟶

DEC. 1, 1951

Dear Mary Alice and John,

I've had the most wonderful mail lately! You should have seen me to know how I felt when I got the most adorable Christmas card I've ever had in my life. That little cowboy has sure grown and does he look sweet and smart. Yes, MA, that is truly our wonderful baby boy. I don't believe I've ever seen anything as cute in my life. I can hardly wait to see our big one done in oil. The snaps also were the best yet. How did you ever manage to get one of him asleep? I can just see him now when he gets tired and decides to rest up a little while. He's a real boy, mama, and we've got to have many more. Too bad the flap on the camera case had to get in the way when Marcus was taking you both together; however, I think it's a good picture anyway. You two sure do look alike. Anybody could sure tell he's your son. I sure like them and whenever you have time, take some more and send them.

The slide rule, along with the plotting pins and stencil pens arrived the day before yesterday, safe and sound as have all the rest you have sent. Thank you ever so much, baby. You might tell Aunt Alice and Uncle Walter that the marking pen is about the best I have ever seen and I am putting it to excellent use. I've marked all my winter gear so now I won't lose any when I have some Gook wash it for me. The Gooks take the clothes by number only. That is, I might send 5 pieces and someone else may send 10. You get back the same number, but gosh only knows whose clothes. Now my name will be in them and there will be no debate. Thank them for me please.

Well we are still in the same positions, and our lines are still holding despite efforts from the NKPA on our left flank trying to push through. The boys are back up in the lines now, and we are in direct support of the 5th Marines. The 1st has gone back in reserve. The peace talks have been sounding good lately and we were ordered by division the other night to fire only when we were under attack and receiving counter battery fire. So now we sit here and fire only 12 rounds in a day. This is our close defensive fire—we adjust them every day.

My boys were out on patrol the other day and shot a spiked buck. We now have him hung up in a tree in the battery and plan to barbecue him Monday. We are going to cook him all day whole over an open pit.

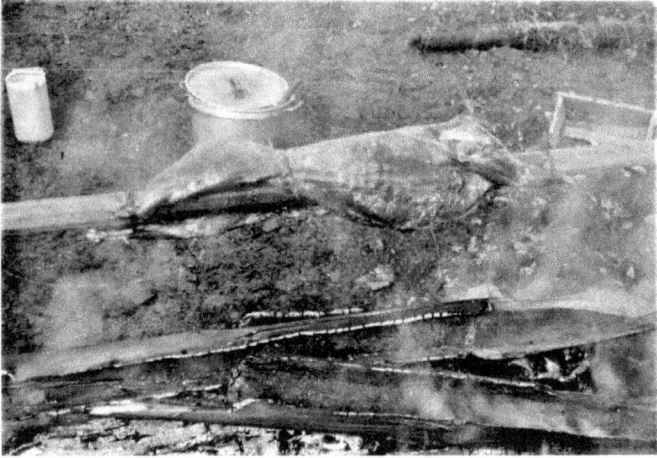

Barbequed venison

Baby, by the time you get this letter it will be fairly close to your birthday. I want to be the first to wish you happy birthday. I sincerely hope that by next year we can both be together and we will never be separated again. Mary Alice, I love you and I always will. You're my sweet little girl. Have a good time, honey, and bake yourself a cake.

I love you, sugar, and someday, top of the "MARK" [InterContinental Mark Hopkins Hotel] in San Francisco, you'll realize I mean every word of it.

Al

P.S. We have had much snow lately and it sure is cold. Love you again.

LETTERS ADDRESSED FROM:

1st Lieutenant A. G. Harris

Headquarters Battery, 2nd Battalion,

11th Marines

1st Marine Division

Fleet Post Office

San Francisco, California

Chapter 11

HEADQUARTERS BATTERY

12 DEC. 1951

Dear Mary Alice,

Well, a lot has happened since I last wrote you. First of all, I am not in Easy Battery any longer. I am now the S-2 in battalion. In the 2nd Battalion, we have a policy of rotating personnel every four months. Well, my time as a battery commander was up December 10 and I was transferred back to the rear with the gear. MA, I had become very attached to my boys in Easy Battery and sure hated to leave. We have all been through a lot together, and we were developed into a smooth working combat outfit. The boys were especially nice to me on the day of my relief, when they came around and shook my hand and said they were proud to serve with me. They gave me a Schafer pen and pencil set, because they said I'd be needing it now. Dammit too, they had sent a boy all the way back to division to get it. They are a swell bunch and I'll always remember the times we had.

My new job on the battalion staff is intelligence officer (S-2); however, I expect it will be changed in a few days to assistant S-3. This is because Captain John Adamson is being transferred from naval gunfire into our battalion. He is not able to stand S-3 duties at the present, simply because he hasn't been working with artillery for some time now and will require some mapping in. He may take over the two's job, and I will be the gunnery officer for the battalion. I'll like this new job very much, because now I can shoot 3 batteries instead of just 1. This new job will not require my presence at the front as my last one often did.

I just got a letter from you, and I'm sure sorry to hear you were not feeling so well. Maybe by now you will be feeling much better. I sure hope by your birthday you will be OK. Have lots of fun, will you? I got two big Christmas packages from you and one from the Norwoods. They all arrived in fine shape and I have opened one from your folks. I was sure taken away by so many separate packages. I hadn't opened any so far until this morning, when my curiosity got the best of me and I opened the package from Mama Bess. It had a little fruitcake in it and boy was it good! Gosh, I haven't tasted anything that good in a long time!! I can hardly wait until Christmas when I can open them all. I also got a letter from Mother which said my brother would more than likely be home for Christmas and that you had said you would meet him in Dallas. Hope you can.

The war has been at a standstill since the peace talks have been going on. Hope a settlement can be reached before long. If they fall through, we will sure go on the attack. We still shoot at them every day to keep them at bay.

Baby, I had better stop now and figure out a metro message so we can shoot better. So good night and sweet dreams. I love you.

Your husband,

Al

⤫

Regarding the pen and pencil set his troops had given him, I imagine Dad was crying when he wrote, "Dammit too, they had sent a boy all the way back to division to get it."

You know this was music to Mom's ears when she read, "This new job will not require my presence at the front as my last one often did." It was welcome news for the whole family, especially during the Christmas season.

I am not sure, but I believe a "metro message" was an official memo from NATO (North Atlantic Treaty Organization) command.

⤫

14 DEC. 1951
0200

Dear Mary Alice and John,

Happy birthday, little girl! You know, down the years past, I can remember several times I have been the first to want to kiss you as you turn another year in your life. I can't do it physically this year, but in my heart, you can bet that I'm thinking of it. Here it is 2 o'clock in the morning and I am standing the FDC watch. I have the 12 to 4 tonight, and I'm sure happy it is half over. This new job is one that should make you happy, because it means that during the watches at night, we do very little shooting unless something breaks. I will have more time to write you. Offhand, if the situation stays the same, I would say you will get a letter almost every day.

Not too much is taking place today. We have fired only a limited number of missions. We are saving up our ammo for a party we have planned for the Gooks soon.

I got a letter from L. D. Jones today. I will enclose it. L. D. could always walk into some good setups. He sure sounds like he wants to go home, but who the hell doesn't!!

I didn't mention in my letter last night about your trip to Jefferson with the McColloms. I'm indeed sorry about little John being sick on the way down, but as I remember back when I was growing up, I did the same. Mama, we have a lot to look forward to. In one of my mother's letters of late, she mentioned a pony they know about around Jefferson and asked if I cared if John had it or one like it when he was old enough for one. Well, of course I don't care! I know every little boy has dreams of someday owning a pony like the cowboys in the shows have. Say, when are you going to start your Christmas shopping for our boy? What is he going to get? Is he going to have a big tree? Come on, woman, tell me!!

Me on the horse (I never got one)

I got a Christmas card from Mrs. McCollom with a long letter about the trip to Jefferson, and also she had enclosed a handkerchief. You might mention it sometime when you see her.

Your raise in pay sounds good but quite small. I, as your husband, think you are worth much more than two dollars a lick. I know it helps out though. Happy to hear you got a Christmas check. I'll bet the party at Lance will be fun. Tell me what you get Sam. Is Rich home yet?

Here in the battalion CP [Christmas party], we have a big 14-foot pine tree set up, and the colonel has asked everyone here to make some type of an ornament to place on it. I've seen all kinds come out of nothing such as beer cans, etc. It's real pretty though.

I expect by this time, Bill Guynes has been by to see you if he stopped on his way to Shreveport. I hope he did, because Bill is a nice fellow and I think you will enjoy talking to him. Also, another boy, Pete Bell from Dallas, left yesterday for the States and he said he would try and see you some Sunday. Boy is he a character.

Well, baby, your old hubby is going to stop now and turn to write his folks a line.

Remember I love you constantly, fully, only, forever, now, then, always, in the future, present and past, and just can't wait until I get you in my arms again. I'll just love you like you ain't never been loved before!

Al

XX

∞⚬∞

Each battery had its own fire direction center (FDC) where target intelligence from the FO was processed and fire direction was given to the Howitzer gun crews. The FO only communicated with the FDC. Headquarters Battery also had an FDC that assisted and coordinated fire from the three batteries in the battalion.[27]

Dad mentioned the following letter from L. D. Jones. L. D. was his fellow officer who got so seasick on the USS William Weigel. It sounds to me like L. D. had won the Korean War lottery. He was definitely a part-time soldier with the ability to travel back and forth to Japan virtually at will. I love his statement that, "It is really nice to be able to come up here and do a little blitz warfare and then get back to Sasebo for some of the better things of life." I wonder what Dad really thought when he read this letter? Dad and L. D. remained good friends after the war and exchanged Christmas cards for many years.

⊂⋙⊃

Yodo Island
Wonsan Harbor
4dec51

Dear Al:

I am out here at present spotting naval gunfire in the bombardment of Wonsan. It is pretty nice as it is not as cold here as in the division area I don't believe, and also we don't move and so we can fix up our quarters pretty good. It is exciting as hell here doing all the shooting and also spotting airstrikes as we have no tactical air party here. Also we go on rides with the Royal Marines up the coast and shoot for them.

Hell with all this war talk, when are we going home? I am off up here where I can never hear any rumor from division. I am under the impression that we should be on the boat that leaves Korea the first of March. Am

I all wet or not? I would surely enjoy getting back on the same ship with you. Is there any possibility that part of the 10th draft might go home in February in your estimation?

I have a pretty good time on this assignment. I spent the first two weeks of November around Japan mainly in Itami, Kyoto, Osaka and saw Sasebo. I came up here on November 14 and have been here ever since. I plan to go back to Japan on about January 20 for some R & R [rest and relaxation], and if you think we might hit the March boat for sure, I'll try to get off there until time to go home. I'm kind of a free operator here as I can go and come to Japan almost at my leisure as long as I don't thoroughly wear out my welcome in Sasebo. It is really nice to be able to come up here and do a little blitz warfare and then get back to Sasebo for some of the better things of life.

You possibly recall the hotel Marunichi in Tokyo where we had the steak. It is under the control of the British, and as I am attached to the British, I am eligible to get reservations there. A close friend of mine, Lieutenant David Ford, of the Royal Marines is going there for two weeks the latter part of January and I plan to unofficially accompany him. Don't say anything about this around the division as I am supposed to be working around here, but I thought you might be interested to know.

Al, drop me a line and let me know your honest opinion on when we can expect to get out of here and back to the States.

Your friend,

LD Jones

∞✕∞

15 DEC. 1951
2100

Dear Mary Alice,

Here it is night again, and I haven't even mailed you the letter I wrote two days ago. I'll drop them all in the mail bag tonight as I go off watch. We now have all the particulars ready for the Gook party [surprise attack]. It will come off at 0200 to 0630 tomorrow morning. Hope we don't have any trouble.

Today, I built a group of shelves for my tent and I'm trying to get my gear squared away after the move.

Captain John Adamson reported in today, and boy did he seem happy about getting into the same battalion I was in. We are the only two boys left out of the 10th draft in this battalion. This may prove to be a great advantage when it comes time for us to go home.

Mary Alice, my executive officer in Easy Battery is Tom Steele. Two days ago, he got word that his wife had a 9 lbs. 2 oz. baby boy. Tom and I have been through a lot together and I would like to do something nice for him and his wife and baby. He already has one two-year-old baby girl. Here is what I would like for you to do. I would like for you to buy an inexpensive baby gift (typical Texan style) and mail it to the baby. Here is his wife's address:

Baby's name: Thomas L. Steele III
1733 Stephen Street
Ridgewood 27 New York

His wife's name is Mrs. T. L. Steele. I would like you to maybe get him some little blue jeans or cowboy shirt or something. It will make them very happy I am sure.

Baby, that's all for tonight and will write again tomorrow.

All my love to you and John,

Al

∞⊗∞

The following is an interesting letter from one of Dad's troops. Apparently, Yon thought he had a run-in with Dad back in Easy Battery, but I think the real purpose of the letter was to see if he could get a two-week leave. As an officer, I'm sure Dad had a wide range of personnel issues to deal with.

∞⊗∞

DEC 15, '51

Dear Lieutenant Harris Sir,

Interpreter Lee is going to go back to battery for his leave. So, I asked him to bring the cot back to Easy Battery. Because I can't get any time to go back after the cot. But I am going to let you know exactly that how came I mistook like that. Because I am afraid that you couldn't get exactly what I meant the other day. For you used to puzzle at my broken expressions that night before I left Easy Battery. Interpreter Kim, as you know, asked you to get him a cot. But you rejected his asking. To tell you the truth, I couldn't stand to hear that conversation anymore. Because I am too chicken-hearted to hear any rejection or to say any rejection against any asking. This is a great defect of mine, and this defect always lets me be pessimistic.

And so, I turn my face to the burning stove and was looking vacantly at it. I didn't know what conversation was going on between you and him. In the end, it was to me as you said "leave the cot in here." So, I thought that you had lent him a cot and you wanted him to return it back to Easy Battery Supply. I didn't think that you meant me because each battery used to issue a cot for its own interpreter. And Easy Battery gave cots or stretchers for the house boys. Those pre-conceptions brought me that mistake. Those are my excuses but true by my God. And if you would allow me to say as follows—I would say I really apologize to you for that mistake and I wish you would forget about that.

Well, be that as it may, the other day I asked you to get me a leave for two weeks—leave on the 27th. I really should like to get that.

Because I got a letter from my brother about half a month ago when I was in Easy Battery. He said that my mother is longing for seeing me and she has been sick for some time and so I want to arrange my leave anyhow. Then I hope any messages from you.

Guess I had better close for now. Goodbye!

Always yours sincerely,

From Yon

ᙢᙢᙢ

16 DEC. 1951

My Dear Mrs. Harris,

And how does this letter find such a lovely and sweet girl today? Fine I hope, because as each day goes by and another one begins, I wish only the best for you and John. Well, as usual, your old man is standing one of the many watches that come around every week. At night, for the past few weeks, the watch standing has been very quiet. The NKPA seem to be taking the peace talks seriously. Either that or they are building up for a push. Everything along the front is very quiet. We are, or rather have been, instructed to take prisoners. Hence, we have been sending out many patrols for that purpose. You remember in my last letter I mentioned a party we had cooked up. Well, that's what it was all about. The patrols went out, but we were pinned down by fire and forced to return without accomplishing the mission. However, we will continue with this action until we do get some for intelligence reports.

Night before last, I had a run-in with a Korean from the KSC (Korean Supply Corp.) who was trying to sell whiskey to some men in our battalion. They turned him over to me and I, in return, wrote out a report and turned him over to the regiment. He only had six bottles of Gook stuff on him. A lot of this whiskey is bad. People have been poisoned and have gone blind as a result of drinking some. We have to keep them out of the area because some of these people around here would sure drink it. By the way, this guy is a South Korean—talks like he has a sweet potato in his mouth. That's the way we tell them apart. Ha Ha!

The mail has been slowed up considerably since the Christmas packages started showing up. However, I was very lucky and got a letter from you this morning. Woman, I want you to get hot and get John's Christmas squared away. I know you stay busy, but, Mama, that boy comes first. Say, honey, you remember the Esquire calendar you sent me some time back. Well, in December, the girl with the red stripe pants—guess what? I want you to get some just like them. Boy that picture sure does remind me of you. I've seen you in that position many times. You know, when I go back through Japan, I'm going to buy you a knocked out set of black skivvies.

That's all for tonight.

Your ever-loving husband,

Al

Chapter 12
CHRISTMAS

The following Christmas cards were mailed from Headquarters Battery in early December, 1951:

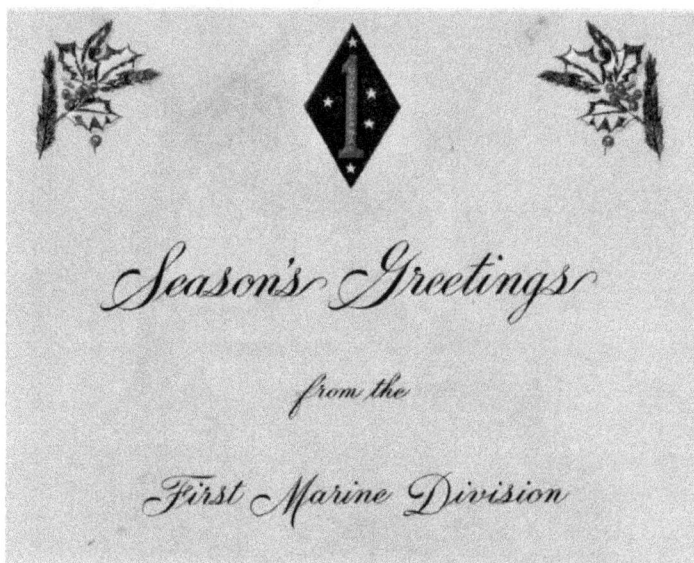

Hi Baby.   5 Dec 51
    How do you like the cards
that were given to us? — I think
they are rather nice don't you.
We also got some others that
different members of the family
will get. Baby, I have
some small gifts that I
will get in the mail soon.
It is really for your birthday
and Christmas together.
John also has a gift — you will
know his from yours.
    I love you + Merry Christmas
                    xx. at.

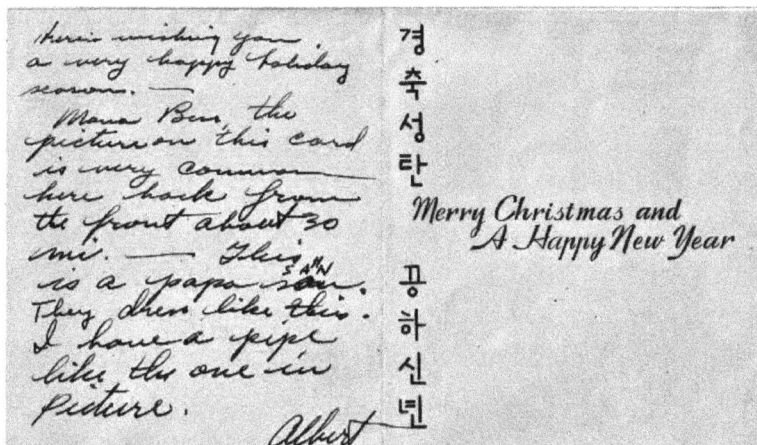

Here is wishing you a very happy holiday season. —— Mama Ben, the picture on this card is very common here back from the front about 30 mi. —— This is a papa san. They dress like this. I have a pipe like the one in picture.

Albert

경
축
성
탄

Merry Christmas and A Happy New Year

공
하
신
년

20 DEC. 1951

Dear Mary Alice,

How do you like this stationery that the special service officer brought around the other day? It is rather colorful don't you think?

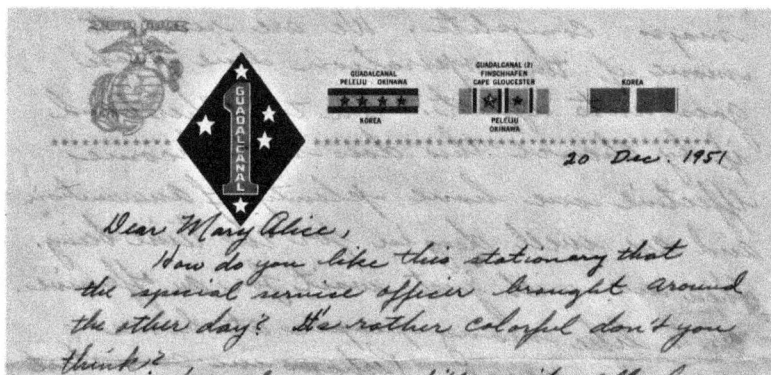

Well, things are still quiet all along the eastern front, and sometimes it is too quiet. However, we are wasting no time in making ready for whatever the future may hold. In the first place, I have told you that the colonel has picked out our position about 8 miles to the rear. This is where the 2nd Battalion will set up if the peace talks go through. Yesterday, the battery commanders went out and selected their positions in that area. All of our survey notes are complete of this area we are in now, so we should be able to zero in on any point in this valley. The operation order is cut, and I have the overlays for our maps complete. We are ready to move if this operation line "peak" goes into effect. On the other hand, if by chance this does not become effective, we have plenty of ammunition and are well dug in for the time being. Then we will just wait for an offensive. We too, like many people at home, pray for peace. Perhaps we can start the new year off with a clean slate as far as blood on the battlefield.

By the time you receive this, Christmas will have come and gone. I don't know what I have been thinking about but the days have certainly gone by fast. I had hoped I would time a letter so that it would arrive in Greenville about the day before Christmas. Nevertheless, baby, I want you to have a wonderful Christmas and know that I am there with you and John. I got your letter telling me of the gifts you plan to give this year. Everything sounds to me like it's the best we have ever done. You are certainly a wonderful little girl to take care of everything like you do. John's toys I'll bet are cute. I only wish that I could be with him when he first sees them. Lila wrote a long letter telling me of her trip home. I'll declare that she spent pages telling me of the things John did while he was with her. Also, she mentioned the little train she and Offie are giving him. Baby, won't he like that!

I too should have a fun Christmas, as you see I have a large package from your folks, a package from Aunt Mary Earle and Theron containing a Mary of Puddin Hill fruitcake, and two great big packages from my cute, darling, blonde wife. I'm going to wait to open them on Christmas eve. Several of us will get together and have Christmas. Lieutenant Steele, Lieutenant Hoben, Lieutenant Russell, Lieutenant Luney and others will gather in our tent and open packages. I'll bet we all have more chow than 40 men could eat. Tom Steele works for the National Biscuit Company (NBC), and they have sent a huge package of all the products they make. The only thing I hope is that we don't get sick eating so much.

I expect that in the next day or two, you will go to Dallas and pick my brother up. I know he will be glad to return home during the holiday season.

It's 0545 now and I've been up since 0400 so I better stop and get to work on the reports I have to turn in to regiment. Baby, I'll be thinking about you now and always, so be sweet, my little girl.

I love you,

Al

23 DEC. 1951

My Darling Wife,

One half a year has come and gone since I last held you in my arms, and that has been caused by the many physical miles between us. The hundreds of miles, that seems so long, are brought to nothing when measured with my heart. And someday, not too far off I hope, we can be so near that I can reach out, and with one quick sweep, draw you near me again. My arms are longing to pull you close, so that I may feel the vibrance of your body, the beating of your heart, and the fullness of your breathing. And also, to look down and gaze into your beautiful brown eyes, and kiss your lips that send out vibrations to make me tingle all over. Yes, and too, the perfume in your hair will be there as you stand, my darling wife, my Athena.

And too, my darling, on my arrival before I have become accustomed to anything, I want to take you away, far away, so that we can live and love and laugh and see. I don't want to be bothered with any small trivial things. I just want you alone for a while.

Someday, darling, where the air is fresh off the Mississippi, and the silver moss is hanging off the cypress by a still bayou, my dreams will come true with you by my side.

Who knows what the New Year will hold for one who loves such a beautiful girl?

All my love,

Always your husband, Al

✖

Do you think Dad was missing Mom? He sure gave it his best in this letter, and you know she cried when she read it. Also, he may very well have had a premonition about the New Year ...

✖

25 DEC. 1951

Dear Mary Alice and John,

It is now 9:25 PM here in Korea, and Christmas day is nearly gone. The time difference between here and Texas is approximately 15 hours, so that would make it about 6:30 AM on Christmas Day for you. I will be on watch from now until twelve. I just want you to know that I'm thinking about you and John and wishing very much that I could be with you. It won't be very long until you and John will jump out of bed and go see what old Saint Nick has left.

This morning I had the 4 to 8 watch, and you can see that I was up early. When I got off, I immediately went in my tent and opened my packages. You see, I was a good boy, except in a few instances, and waited until Christmas to see what I had. Darling, I was never so surprised in all my life as I was when I saw all the individually wrapped packages. They were all done so pretty and nice. I got a charge out of the cute cards along with them. You are just swell, that's all! It seems to me that I have seen some of the boxes you wrapped some of the things in before. Take for instance the iron box and the box John's cowboy boots came in. I told the boys of the history of each, and also, I am saving the iron box and may send something in it later. The things you sent are just out of this world to me. I can certainly use each and every item. I got a big kick out of the four bars of soap John sent. It couldn't be that his mother had anything to do with that, could it? Also, the toilet articles are welcome, because we just don't have anything like that over here. Baby, the book you sent, *Garden in My Heart*, is just the finest present I got nearly. Thanks a million for everything. Tell your mom and dad thanks too. It was all just too good to be true.

Honey, about the packages I told you some time ago that I was sending—well I haven't mailed them yet simply because I was unable to find any wrapping material. I used, this morning, some of the wrapping of the packages I opened. They should be in the mail tomorrow. I stuck in some things that I will want to keep for a while after I return home. You can look them all over but I do want you to save them for me. There are two packages in all. I say that so you will know when shipment is complete.

When Christmas day started off this morning, there was no snow on the ground whatsoever except on the mountain sides. Now everything is covered in a blanket of white about 1 foot deep. It is still snowing hard too.

The noon meal was everything it should be. We had shrimp cocktail with sauce, coleslaw, corn, green peas, Irish spuds, sweet spuds, turkey and dressing, hot bread, olives, nuts, candy, coffee, ice cream, fruit cake, pumpkin pie, and mincemeat pie. Gosh, so much I can hardly remember it all. Anyway, it sure was good. After chow, Lieutenant Russell and I went back to the rear about 8 miles to a show. Paul

Douglas and Jan Sterling were the main attractions. They put on a good show. They did part of the show "Born Yesterday." This was very funny because they did some ad-libbing on many of the lines to make them sexier. Boy, and what they didn't get away with isn't in the books! At the end, Jan Sterling jumped down in the audience and started kissing all the boys. There are many boys around here that won't wash their faces for some time now! All in all, the show was outstanding out there in the snow. No, baby, I didn't get my face all messed up, I was too far away.

Sugar, be sure and write all the details about Christmas. You know I want to hear them. I got a very cute card from Aunt Nona and Roy. Also, a cute letter inside. And Nona sure does like you a lot.

Baby, I better stop for now and look my new book over some more.

All my love to you my darling, and may I see you and John soon.

Love, XX

Al

Chapter 13

1952

2 JANUARY 1952

My Dear Mary Alice and John,

I am feeling rather blue tonight simply because I haven't heard from you in over a week now. I know it is not your fault though, because this mail situation since Christmas has been fouled up. The mail calls have been few and far between. Maybe by tomorrow I will get a whole stack, and I know life will be a bed of roses. I might mention also that I have yet to receive Mother's Christmas package.

Since I last wrote you, the new year has come and gone, or is still here with us I had better say. We had a very fun time on New Year's Eve. First of all, a wonderful meal, then the movie (*Painting the Clouds with Sunshine*). After the show, we all got together for a beer and saw the new year in. You should see the show I mentioned above. It was very good, but sure nearly gave a whole bunch of Marines a heart attack. The gal in it just shook it around a little too much. (Excuse please, but I just ran out of ink.)

We are now shooting more than we have been. At night, we shoot what we call TOTs (time on target). The reason for this is as follows: from intelligence reports, we get such information as enemy strong points, assembly areas, mess areas, command posts, etc. Now after gathering all information concerned, we mass all the artillery we have in this valley on the target at a certain time. The objective is to have a great volume of fire on a concentrated point at one time, hence the abbreviation TOT. So much for the shop talk.

This new job doesn't keep me as busy as my last one did. I've even had time to read two books. One written by Mickey Spillane called *Vengeance is Mine.* This is a thriller of a detective story. Mike Hammer is a rough and ready character. I also read a love story about the old south called *The Vixens.* They were both pretty good. If you ever have time, you should read them. However, I expect you will always be busy and never have time.

By what I am about to write, you may think your husband is still a child at heart. Anyway, since it has been so cold, the mice have invaded our tents. I have tried to think of some way to rid the tent of them without taking out my .38 and blasting them off the walls. You see, it causes too many holes. So, I have made myself a slingshot and I am becoming quite expert with it. I haven't killed a rat as yet. Maybe this practice in making things like slingshots and things like that will be good, because I know I have to help a little boy do it.

Honey, I got to wondering what it would be like to have you and John around close. You know, I'll bet I won't even know our boy! I just wonder and wonder how his voice sounds, what he talks about, and how it would be to have you both around close to me.

Well, baby, it's 2400. So good night and I love you.

Al

∽⟨⟩⟨⟩⟨⟩⟨⟩∾

Can you imagine being in a gathering with your fellow soldiers and suddenly you hear eighteen (or more) artillery shells come screaming into your location? Time on target (TOT) was a technique developed by the British Army in North Africa at the end of 1941. It proved very successful and has been a standard artillery practice since. It requires a substantial amount of coordination between the firing batteries because of the different distances and trajectories required. The general military standard is for the artillery rounds to simultaneously land in a three-second time frame.[28]

I can't tell you how many slingshots Dad and I made while I was growing up—it was a bunch! Once I was older, I started buying the professionally made ones that were extremely powerful. When my wife and I moved to Ohio, one of the first things I did was teach my grandchildren how to make a slingshot from branches we cut down in our backyard. Dad would have been pleased!

SUNDAY 6 JANUARY 1952

Dear Mary Alice,

I am feeling much better than I was when I last wrote you, because yesterday I got the letter I had been waiting for. When I don't get mail from you, something seems to go wrong with me and I don't operate right. I guess you are just the one vital part in my life that makes me click.

I was so happy to find out about our boy's Christmas. My, didn't he get a lot of nice toys! I'll bet he was a happy little fellow. You said in your letter that John was in bed beside you saying he wished I could come home and that he loved me. Well, you tell him that I certainly love him and as soon as I can leave, I'll be right home. I often close my eyes and try and picture it in my mind, you and John playing, eating, sleeping, etc. I can draw a very clear picture of you (MA) but I can't quite get John. I guess it is because I know he is changing very rapidly and I can only remember some months back.

Well, I see you now have your old job back. I sure hope you like it. You should get another raise, shouldn't you? Baby, the last week or two we have gotten quite a number of officers in the regiment. However, they are infantry and will have to go through a training course before they can relieve some of our boys. After they take formation, your old man will be right at the top of the list to go home. February and March will tell but I expect it will be April before I leave. Mama, tell John that Lava soap is a sure thing for getting that rough dirt out.

That's all for now so be sweet.

I love you two.

Your husband,

Al

⊶⋈⊷

10 JANUARY 1952

My darling blonde wife and John,

I got a long typed letter from you dated December 30 that brought me up-to-date on what went on over the Christmas holidays. It sure sounds as though you had a good time. In answer to some of your questions, I can now say that I am approximately 500 yards to the rear of where I used to be and in another draw. Everything is going along fine, very quiet until last night and tonight. The Gooks have started up shelling again. They don't throw in much volume of fire, but what they do is accurate. One man in the 3rd Battalion was hit pretty bad and was evacuated this morning at 0340 by plane. Outside of this, nothing much has happened.

I too got quite a number of Christmas cards—a lot of them from my former students at Quinlan. I imagine Dorothy Cox had a lot to do with that. I didn't send out very many cards but of those that I did, only one was returned. Uncle Les's card was returned to me. The reason was I didn't have the proper address on it. Would you send it to me please? I'll try and write him a letter.

The mixer you got us sounds good. I hope I can soon use it with you. However, I just can't think of very many mechanical things that

170

would interest me with you around. You are going to have trouble with me, little lady!

I got the Lance paper with your picture in it and, woman, you sure do look cute. It was mighty nice to see a picture that had so many familiar faces in it. I'll be waiting until I get the pictures you took of John on Christmas. I'll bet they are all good. How has the car been running lately?

Baby, I've been thinking about what we are going to do when I get back to the States and time comes for me to get out of the Marine Corps in June. I've sort of considered maybe extending for a year and asking for duty in California or in Fort Sill. What would you think of this? Or maybe even some East Coast duty would be good. The reason I am considering this is because I don't know anything else I could make more money at right now, do you? I fully expect to make captain before long, and when I do, we would be able to get along fairly well on what I would make. I might even swing a deal where I could get stationed in Corpus Christi or most anywhere. Now, I've just been thinking about this. What do you think? Perhaps we shouldn't do this at all, but tell me, will you?

Well, sugar, I better stop now and write my folks a line. I haven't written them in some time now.

Baby, take care of yourself and our boy John.

I love you.

Al

14 JAN. 1951
0445

To a cute little blonde that has a boy by the name of John,

Hi, honey! How are you this morning? I hope you feel a lot better than you did when you wrote me the letter I got yesterday (January 6). I'm very sorry you have had a cold that has bothered you so much. Take care of yourself. I guess I have been lucky so far, because I haven't been sick since I arrived here.

I sure liked your last letter with the pictures of John's Christmas. All of them were cute as they could be. I like the one with his granddaddy very much.

You ask about my knowing when I might come home. Baby, that is still very hard to tell, but you can feel sure I will let you know in plenty of time so you can quit out at Lance.

I love Dad

Two of my interpreters came back off Christmas leave, and each one brought me a present. I got a brass ashtray with a design in the top that stands for something in the universe. Also, Peter Yu brought a small handkerchief to me and said, "Send it to my Mrs." He also gave me a small ROK flag. I will be sending them on to you soon. I may send you my riding crop with a Gook pipe when I do. The pictures that you will find enclosed are some that were taken by my jeep driver. He gave them to me a few days ago.

That's all for now.

I love only you.

XX, Al

⌒✕⌒

20 JANUARY 1952
0041

Mary Alice and John,

Here it is in the wee hours on the morning of the 20th, and I find myself writing to you sweet people again. It seems that I have been sending you quite a few pictures of myself lately, but I just can't help it, because someone is always giving me one that they took way back then. This one, this time, was taken on approximately September 14, 1951. We had just taken the hill that I am on (Hill 749). The two rifles that are slung over my left shoulder are Russian made jobs that were left by the retreating enemy. I brought them back to the battery for some of my forward observers. Our lines are now only about 1,000 meters from this point.

About the most exciting thing that has happened around here lately is a mysterious enemy tank that has appeared in the lines. It is a funny thing, but no one had heard it, and only a few people have seen it. I'm beginning to believe they are clutched up and seeing things.

Dad on Hill 749

Our air observers have looked and haven't reported any signs of one. But who knows; maybe one is up there in the hills. It's been snowing here off-and-on all day yesterday. It's not too cold either, and I don't seem to mind it at all.

I'll go off watch here at 0400, and then I'll have to get up again at 0700 to go see the colonel. He phoned last night and said he wanted to see me at that time. I don't have any idea as to what it's about, but I imagine it could be about an investigation I held concerning the burning of a tent the other night. In our ordinance section, a homemade stove exploded and burned the tent down along with approximately $2,000 worth of gear. He (the colonel) wanted an investigation held to see if there was any dereliction of duty.

Mama, if John is saying all the things you say he is, he is getting to be quite a talker. I just can't imagine at all. It's sure going to be nice being home with you two.

I got my Christmas package from Mother the other day and boy were the cookies good. I had never tasted anything like them before in my life.

Well, baby doll, I had better close for now and say—

"Say good-looking—what you got cooking—and how about cooking something up with me. I've got a hot rod Ford and a two-dollar bill and I know a little place just over the hill—say good looking, how about cooking something up with me."

So, bye now,

Love,

Al XX

∞✕∞

After all this time, they were still less than a mile from Hill 749.

∞✕∞

28 JANUARY 1952

Dear Mary Alice and John,

You two cute people have been asking me in your letter when I can expect to leave Korea. Well, the answer to that is not in clear view as yet, but here is the latest prospect. By the end of this month, everyone up to the seventh draft will be on their way home. We did not get many officers in between the seventh and tenth draft. In the battalion,

I stand fifth on the rotation list. In the regiment, I stand about 35th on the list. Now, if we continue to get people in like we have been, 35 at a whack, there is a possibility that I could leave here around March 15. Now, baby, don't count on this at all because I just can't tell exactly when, but when I can tell better there will be plenty of time to let you know. Tom Steele says I will leave around March 1, but I think he is just daydreaming. Kind of makes me feel good though.

The pictures you enclosed in your last letter are just as cute as they can be. I know John is as cute acting as his pictures are cute. I'll be home to see him one of these days. That first picture where you and he are standing together is just as beautiful as I will ever see. A beautiful mother and her son. Baby, I must say that you haven't lost any of your allure. Just a picture of you makes my breath grow short, my heart beat twice as fast, along with a yearning to hold you in my arms. Baby, I could have looked this world over from top to bottom and could never have found anyone that sends me into a whirl like you do. I don't know whether or not I've ever told you, but I certainly should have. I often give thanks for having you as my wife and mother of my children (future). I love you, Mary Alice.

I got into a funny situation the other day with a few of my fellow officers. One guy made a statement that he thought the sexiest women in the world were school teachers. Of course, this was disputed by the battalion doctor who thought nurses were. They thought that they could settle the situation by asking Lieutenant Scollary (he is married to a nurse) and myself who seemed to meet the situation at hand and able to give a full discussion on the subject. We finally decided that wives were the sexiest people anywhere!

I hadn't realized that we had around $1,000 in the bank. I think you have done absolutely great at saving! I hadn't expected so much. Yes, I have saved a little money over here. I now have about $350 on the books. By the time I leave, I expect to have around $500 or $600. I may send you $100 before long because I'll have it in cash. When I do, you can put it in the bank or spend it, whichever you like. That is just for being my sweet wife.

Now get set for what I'm about to tell you. Ready, here goes, you asked for it. I bought an 8mm Revere movie camera for $127. It is the latest model out, magazine load, triple turret with telephoto and 1.9 lens. It has a $20 carrying case. This runs around $200 in the States. Along with this I bought a GE [General Electric] light meter for $19 (sells for $32.50 in the States). I've taken two rolls of film with it and have three more to use up. Now I know we could probably do without it, but I think in years to come the full appreciation will come forth. If by chance you think we shouldn't keep it, I can certainly sell it for much more than I paid. I've been offered $150 and could get $175 for it. But the light meter, I will not sell it! If we keep it, we will next have to get us a projector. The film (50 feet) runs $2.80 per roll which includes processing. Think it over and tell me what you think.

While you are having spring-like weather, we are having cold and snowy weather here. I am making it OK, except for the fact that moisture is freezing in my mustache. I may have a picture for you soon. You never have seen it, have you? By the way, have you ever been kissed by a man with a mustache? If not, you better stand by because you're going to be. I am enclosing some more pictures—two are of the formation I had in Easy Battery when the regimental colonel (Hemphill) came down to present awards. The other is of the deer we killed and barbecued.

Colonel Hemphill presenting awards to Easy Battery

Dad is second from the left in the background

Well, darling, it is late and I had better stop for now.

I love you as ever.

Al, XX

∞✕✕∞

So, Mom never gave Dad permission to buy the movie camera, and he finally just purchased it! Of course, it was already worth more than he paid for it, and they would come out ahead financially if she still nixed the purchase. He was sure getting a little desperate for her approval, but he had his camera!

∞✕✕∞

2 FEB. 1952

Dear Mary Alice,

Baby doll, here it is, the second month already of the new year. I sure hope time flies between now and the time I leave here. Say, with February coming on, we have several events to remember, don't we? First, we have Valentine's Day, next our anniversary, and then Mother's birthday. This month we will have been married six years—yes! Baby, you have made each and every one happier than I have ever been in my life.

Would you please get Mother a small remembrance from us?

I am enclosing a few small snaps that one of the boys took one night of the search lights. The lights are employed for the purpose of lighting up the enemy lines so we can tell what is going on. Anyway, you can see a glimpse of what we see at night over here.

Night search lights

Since I last wrote you, we had a very bad accident happen. One of our own planes got fouled up as to where he was and came down and strafed and bombed us. He dropped six bombs, two 1,000 pounds and four 250 pounds. We had only one boy hit by a machine gun bullet. He is in the Fox Battery. The 7th Marines had the bombs drop in their area and several people were injured. The pilot cracked up in the enemy territory after this happened. No one has determined how the mistake was made. There are so many reasons why one should be able to tell that this is not enemy country. Anyway, it was pretty bad.

I haven't heard from you in several days now, and I'm wondering if everything is OK. I sure hope you haven't had any more colds. I've had the 0400 to 0800 watch this morning, and it's now about chow time. I'll quit for now—I just hope I get a letter from you today.

I love you, sweet,

Al

3 FEB. 1952

Dear MA and John,

As usual, the day after I write you and say I haven't been getting any mail, I get a letter that very next day. I too, just look and look for your letters.

The time is very definitely running out for me here, but it can't go fast enough. I still can't tell you anything for sure as to the exact time, but I'm hoping for March. Needless to say, as you have said, time will move very slow from now on. Sugar, if and when I leave here, I expect to have some time in Japan to do a little shopping around. I will sure try and get you the things you want me to. As of now, you have requested some lacquered bowls, boxes (one inside the other), pictures on silk, and boy-oh-boy, a Japanese kimono. The last article will be fun to pick out, as well as the rest, but I may get a bigger kick out of this. Say, baby, before I come home, if there is anything else that you want me to try and get, just tell me and I'll do my best.

Honey, I was sure sorry to hear that John has been ill. You take care of him I know. I can hardly believe I get to see him sometime in the near future.

I expect before very long, I will be sending some of my things home to you. I have some odds and ends that I would like to keep. Have you received the package I sent before? I will also send two of my parkas with the package. I don't know where I will wear these right now, but I'm sure we can find some use for them. It is too cold at the present to send them now. From what the groundhog saw today, it looks as though we will have six weeks more of winter.

Honey, I still don't know what I should do about getting out or staying in the Corps for maybe a year. We could save some money by staying in for a while. If I stayed in, we could probably get a station most anywhere we would like. I could even get stationed in Japan, I imagine. What would you think of that? I know you probably can imagine all kinds of things, but really, it's not as bad as you think. If you could be with me, it would sure be good. I know you would get a kick out of something like that. Now don't get worried, because I'm not going to do anything rash until I've talked with you and have taken my 30-day leave.

Baby, it's nearly 2400 and I will soon go off watch. I won't know how to act without staying up half the night!

So goodnight, sweetheart—I love you.

Al

❀

It had been fifty-four days since Dad moved back to the Headquarters Battery. In general, things had been going smoothly, and Dad had written Mom sixteen letters, or about one every three days. Dad was talking about coming home, possibly in March—one short month away. He was thinking that maybe he should stay in the Corps and perhaps they could even be stationed in Japan. Regardless, he would have a thirty-day leave when he got home and they could decide what to do.

1952

And then the letters stopped. Mom wouldn't receive a letter for two weeks. I'm sure she was becoming extremely distressed ...

Chapter 14
HILL 884

Dear Mary Alice and John,

By the time you receive this letter, it will have been a long time since you have heard from me. I offer no excuses except I've been rather busy. To explain further, I am now an artillery liaison officer with the 7th Marines. I am located on top of Hill 884 in icy North Korea. I am with the right flank battalion on the front. I came up February 8. I am with a good bunch of men here, and I like it very well. It has been snowing for the past few days, and we are simply snowed in. There is snow all over the place. I've been so busy getting things squared away around here to suit me, that I just haven't had much time for anything else.

Two days after I came up, we went into Operation Clam-Up. This is where we faked a relief of lines and went into our holes and didn't come out except at night. What we were trying to do was have the enemy come up to our positions and then we would try and capture them. We were not to shoot until you could see the whites of their eyes. We did exactly that and believe me we had some time. They only came around at night blowing bugles, etc. Operation Clam-Up lasted six days. I slept most of the day and stayed awake at night. This is the reason for my not writing as I have been.

I guess you are wondering why I'm up here. The only reason that I have is the new colonel of our battalion said he wanted more experienced men in the liaison jobs. I'll be here until March 10 (Texas Independence Day) at which time I'll go into reserve for about 20 days. I doubt that I'll come back up on the hill after that. Because by then, I'll almost be ready to sail for home. Right now, I plan to leave around April 10–15. I can hardly wait until they say go. It won't be long though, baby. Since the snow and Operation Clam-Up, I haven't had much mail myself. I got two letters from you through yesterday. It just really makes a guy feel good to hear from his loved ones. The way you describe John and his actions sure make him sound like a little character. I know he must be sweet and keeps you in stitches with his talking. I really can't imagine it. Can he do all that talking you say he can? I'm glad you got my packages. The Korean boys and girls do not wear the little shoes for overshoes. That is what they wear in the summer. In the winter, they wear a shoe that looks like a tennis shoe. The spoons were bought in Won-ju and are called edie-wa spoons. The Koreans we have around here eat rice with them. They also use chopsticks too. Baby, will you make me up a list of what you want in Japan and send it to me?

In my moving around, I may have lost my little book that I had everything in. Get me something that I can fold up and put in my billfold. I'll try and get everything you want. Honey, when I come home, do you plan to meet me at the West Coast? If so, how? Do you plan to drive out or fly? We had better start making plans. Sugar, I had better close now because I have to make up an overlay to submit to the S-3.

I believe yesterday was our wedding anniversary. Sorry I couldn't send roses, but I'll try to make up for it somehow. I love you, baby.

Al

∞✕∞

Although his letters did not reveal a lot of war news, there is little doubt that Dad was highly productive during his time at Headquarters Battery. That was who he was. During Dad's command, I'll bet Easy Battery was the best in the battalion. Dad had already proved himself in battle and he commanded the respect and loyalty of his troops. He was a multi-talented officer/soldier that you could depend on, and he stood out to his superiors. The war demanded performance from the artillery battery on Hill 884, and Dad was sent there to make sure it happened. Hill 884 was located in the Punchbowl area.

Operation Clam-Up lasted February 10-15, 1952. By stopping all air strikes, artillery fire, and ground patrols, the UN hoped to convince the KPA that their troops had withdrawn from their lines so that significant numbers of enemy soldiers could be captured. The KPA was not deceived

*and instead moved supplies and reinforcements to the front
lines, thereby strengthening their overall position.[29]*

*I am sure Mom flipped when she read this letter. Dad was
back on the front and talking about "not shooting until you
see the whites of their eyes." The last time he was on a hill
was unspeakable. She and Dad were starting to plan his return home. What was the Marine Corps thinking? Mom
was no pushover, and I'm sure she was mad as hell.*

*Ever the optimist, Dad pushed the expected "leave" date to
around April 10-15 and wanted to know how they planned
to meet when he returned to the States. He knew this letter
would come as a shock, and he was trying to make the best
of the situation.*

∝✕✕◦

24 FEBRUARY '52
SUNDAY

Dear Mary Alice and John,

I've just got to stop for a few minutes and write you dear sweet people.
Your husband has been very busy with his job of fighting Gooks. I've
been on this hill seventeen days and am becoming very tired of the
C-rations [canned pre-cooked combat meal] we are eating. We have
one hot meal per day and that is served at 10 AM in the morning. I
am now with the 1st Battalion 7th Marines, as they, today, relieved the
2nd Battalion 7th Marines. For the past four or five days, we have had

some trouble with the enemy as they are probing our lines consistently. We have gotten out rather light though, only two KIA and one WIA.

Honey, I have had several letters from you lately and sure did enjoy them. I also got the cute valentine from John and his letter. Funny thing, but I can almost read it. The valentine you sent was swell. Also, the anniversary card was the cutest I've ever seen.

Baby doll, the clothes you are buying sound swell, and I expect you to have lots by the time I arrive. I mean lots of them! I'm still planning on leaving around April 10-15 so be ready. I got a valentine from Mother and Dad with a handkerchief in it. It had sachet. It reminded me of many other lovely smells I've had before around you. The day I meet you on the dock, you had better have some bewitching perfume on that will just knock me over.

Write what you think you will do on my return to the States. If you would come out to the coast, we could have a wonderful second honeymoon back to Texas. I will have some leave coming up you know. You could fly out, and we could go to Mexico City for a while and then home. I'm just daydreaming. Write what you think.

Maybe I better stop for now—will write again soon.

Love,

Al

∞✕∞

It was another week before Mom got this letter. Dad had been very busy fighting the North Koreans, and they had really gotten off pretty light—only two KIA and one WIA. I'm sure from Mom's point of view, this was exactly how soldiers died just before they were scheduled to come home.

In 1951, a new, improved C-ration was introduced. It was a meal in a tin can, had a visible solder seam, and incorporated an opening strip with a key that was soldered to the base of the can. A variety of entrees included chopped eggs and ham, pork and beans, and meat chunks and beans. There were several other components typically consisting of five crackers, packets of instant coffee and powdered milk, sugar, a cocoa disc, and a tin of jam. There was also a separate can of fruit which Dad said was highly prized, especially the peaches.[30]

Field cooking equipment was not required for a C-ration; however, in **Devotion,** *Adam Makos describes a soldier in the Battle of Chosin Reservoir remarking to his sergeant, "I've already got breakfast cooking," as he patted his side where he had tucked a box of C-rations beneath his parka.*[31] *I'll bet Dad did that, too.*

∞✕∞

8ᵀᴴ MARCH 1952

Dear Mary Alice and John,

Honey babe, I just this minute finished reading a letter from you. In some parts, it made me feel very bad for not writing you. I thought to myself that I had better just take time out and write. This job with the infantry sure keeps me jumping. This job is a 25 hour a day job with no time off for lunch. Our mission here is to keep making constant contact with the enemy and to capture them where we can. We took a prisoner yesterday around noon. It's cold, the work is continuous, and we are always having duels with artillery, mortars and light firearms. Had some bad luck two days ago when three FO officers were hit. One of the boys was from San Angelo—he was killed. At all times, it is dangerous over here, but as I see it, if one plays it cool, his chances are much better. I won't come off this hill until March 14 now due to the bad luck we had. When I do, I will be in reserve for 20 days. (375519) This number here is one that I just took down as to where a round just came in. This was an 82.

As to my coming home, they have fouled up very bad as far as I can see in the respect that they are having to send men back to the States to let them out of the Corps. Up to now, seven boys have gone back that just got here in September and two in October. Now, since they are going home, someone has to stay. It just doesn't seem right though to see them come and go and all you do is stay. This month, there is no scheduled rotation draft of officers to leave for the States. But the colonel is trying to fly the boys out that should leave. If they do go, I will more than likely go the same way in April. However, this is all to take place in the future. It will have to materialize before I believe it. It'll work out for the best anyway, honey, so don't worry. I had better get busy and just wanted you to know I'm OK. You know your daddy will keep his head down.

Love you,

Al, XX

P.S. Baby, you can feel sure that I will call you as soon as I leave Korea. The 30 days that I have when I return sure is going to be spent well. Write me where you would like to go.

Love again,

Al

∞✕∞

Another twelve days passed and Mom got this letter. More Marines were dying, and to top it off they were sending soldiers home that arrived in Korea well after Dad did. I'm sure Mom was livid. Dad didn't like it either, but he was a soldier and would do what was necessary.

Also note that Dad took down a six-digit number locating the point where an 82 mm Russian mortar shell had just hit in the area. The number was a grid reference of the area surrounding the battery, just like they used when shooting artillery rounds. It was important information for the officer in charge to know.

Chapter 15
SEOUL

27 MARCH 1952

Dear Mary Alice and John,

You dear sweet people, here is what has been happening to your daddy. The last letter I wrote you, was on the top of Hill 884 in icy North Korea on the Eastern front. Well, I thought I would never get off there. We stayed up a total of 50 days. That is about as long as anyone has ever been up at one time without having a break. I ate C-rations until I just couldn't stand to even smell them. Anyway, the day finally came up for all people to move off the lines and be relieved by the ROK. The day was very bad with much driving snow and wind. Even some of the Koreans coming up had their hands frozen. Anyway, it was about a 3½ mile hike to the rear command post. I had managed to get a plane ride (egg beater) down for some of my boys. This was arranged through the air officer who is a good friend of mine from Yangoo Valley. The night we were ready to move off, and it was around 8 PM, because the infantry had gone during the day and we were the last ones to move off. As the copters were coming in and taking the boys out five at a time, I got word to stay on the hill that night in case they needed to use our artillery. Well, I need to tell you that I did not sleep a wink that night with those people. They could understand very little English, and I don't know to this day what I would have done had we had an attack.

Anyway, nothing happened that way. But I did have a start. About 4 AM in the morning, I was sort of dazed because of lack of sleep, when I looked up and saw the place (bunker) was all in flames. I grabbed my belongings and hauled out of the place. The two Koreans that were with me put it out in short time, and everything went smooth. The next day, the colonel had a copter come and get me, and by noon, I was in Headquarters Battery having chow. That afternoon, we pulled out of the area and headed for the western sector and that is where I am now writing you from.

I am now located about 20 miles above Seoul. I am very close to where they are having the peace conference. The situation here is quite different than it was in the Eastern front. The hills here are much smaller than the ones we came out of—the tallest one being around 100 meters. The natives are living all around us. This seems strange, because before we had never seen any in the other area. I am taking many pictures that I do hope turn out well. I also know you will get a bang out of the way people live. It is very primitive.

Baby, about my coming home, I just can't figure it out. So many boys who came over way after I did have left. It's not right, but everything will work out OK. I'll just keep on doing my job and someday it'll just come out of the clear blue. In the back of my head, I keep saying I'll make it next month though.

Sweet, you are the one and only—the mother of our boy, John. I love you, darling. I want you so bad it hurts. This move we have made has taken some time, and mail both ways has been fouled up. I'll write you about a week before I leave here, and the letter should arrive before I get there, provided I don't fly. Anyway, I'll let you know what to expect. I'll take care of myself and hurry home as fast as I can.

I love you,

Al

⚬⚬⚬⚬⚬

These must have been extraordinarily tough times for Mom. It was another nineteen days before she received this letter. Can you imagine day after day with no news and no way to get any? She could have received a wire from the Red Cross at any time and, of course, there was the dreaded knock on the door from Marine Corps representatives.

I have heard this story on more than one occasion from family members. I'm sure everyone rallied around Mom to help her get through the stress. Dad's exit from Hill 884 was extraordinary, but at least he was now twenty miles north of Seoul and there were natives living in the area. He was taking a lot of pictures, and I get the feeling from reading his letter that the overall situation was relatively peaceful.

Unfortunately, the prospect of his coming home had faded,
but something still told him it would be in the next month ...

∞✕✕∞

APRIL 7, 1952

Dear Mary Alice and John,

I've been busy as usual because this man's Marine Corps can find job
after job for one to do. Since I came off Hill 884, in the Eastern sector,
I haven't had a bit of rest. A few days after we left the east and occupied the line sector in front of Seoul, the KMC had a 500-man probe
and the 3rd Battalion 7th Marines was alerted to be committed in the
line. At that time, I was approximately 14 miles from this battalion. I
was awakened at 1:15 in the morning and was told that I was to join
them in the attack to return lost ground. I got all my boys together and
took off with nothing but a battle map and a compass to guide me. I
arrived at 4 AM, only to find out the alert had been called off. The
KMC reserve battalion had pushed them back and had the situation
well in hand! I'm certainly glad we were not called on.

The next day, I went back to my unit, fully expecting to get the word I
would be leaving Korea on or about the 10th of this month. Instead, I
found out they had a liaison job for me on the Gimpo Peninsula. This
is where I am now. Baby, it's the same old story. I have been declared
essential to the effort and will be unable to leave until May 10, or
thereabouts. They will have to get me out of here or else—I do have
the word of Colonel Thomas that I will leave then. I have the distinc-
tion, if you want to call it that, of being the oldest hand in the battalion.

Baby, I've counted so hard on coming home this month that it's like being kicked in the teeth knowing different, but now I've more or less accepted it. The only hard part now is telling you. I know everything will work out OK. Please try and understand, darling. The colonel said he could tell me OK, but was certainly glad he didn't have to tell our wives.

Darling, when I came over here to Gimpo, I had to go through Seoul. This is quite an experience and I did see many places I had wanted to see. Seoul has very many beautiful buildings and I wish I did have time to look them all over good. Perhaps I can take some pictures and can tell you the full story sometime.

Baby, I got your letter with the enclosed letter about the school teaching job in Tyler. This sounds pretty good to me, but I think I should wait until we can be together before I commit myself in any way. There are many things in this world that we three can do. I just want to spend the rest of my life making you happy.

Baby, I've been out on reconnaissance all day, and I'm mighty tired. What's more, I'll have to go all day tomorrow. So, I expect I better hit the sack. I don't exactly remember when I last wrote Mother, but will you let them know that everything is OK for me. If I have time, I will write one of these nights. Give John a big kiss from his daddy, and tell him I will see him soon.

Love from your husband,

Al

❦

So much for the peaceful setting twenty miles north of Seoul. Can you imagine being awakened at 1:15 a.m. and being told to get your men together and join in a major attack on the enemy some fourteen miles away? It was pitch dark, and there wasn't a road to where you were going. With only a battle map and a compass, you were to head off over the hills to a place you probably hadn't been before. No doubt about it: this was definitely how a soldier got killed in the twilight of his duty.

But Dad had faced adversity many times before, and he would do it again. I'm sure the relief he felt when he got there and did not have to fight was overwhelming. The trip back was a hell of a lot easier.

Dad had been declared essential to the war, and he wouldn't be going home in April. They had another liaison job for him on the Gimpo Peninsula (across the river from Inchon), and his discharge was now postponed until around May 10. The most positive thing he had was the word of Colonel Thomas that the 10ᵗʰ was a good date.

Chapter 16
GIMPO PENINSULA

Dear Mary Alice and John,

At last, what do you know. I have had the afternoon off. This is the first time I can remember that happening in a long time. This morning I went to church. The service was as nice as can be expected here in the field. In some respects, it was even more beautiful than many of the large church services. What I mean by that is, the setting being among the hills, low and rolling, turning green and dotted ever so much with a wild lavender flower. Even though the place I left was very cold, Spring has begun here just above Seoul. I have thought much today about what we did last Easter and how different this one has been. Did you and John go to Sunday school? I'll bet you two look pretty this morning. I remember so well our going to church last Easter in Oceanside. Here's hoping you had a wonderful Easter day.

Sugar, I guess you are wondering about my return. Well, I'm wondering too. The scuttlebutt has it that there will be a draft leaving here around April 25. If I'm lucky, I'll be on it. I'm almost positive we will leave by boat from Inchon and go to Japan. When I reach Japan, I will cable you when I expect to be either in San Francisco or San Diego. Boy, I can hardly wait to leave.

Baby, I've been thinking about extending for two months, after I take my leave. You can extend for any length of time one wishes to. It could mean a vacation for both of us and maybe a little extra money. I believe this would be better than just lying around the house. However, I'm not doing a thing until I get my feet on U.S. soil.

This job here on Gimpo is quite different than the ones I have had before. I am teaching a school on the conduct of fire and survey. I get a bang out of it. The Hahn River is between us and the enemy, so I don't worry much about that. It doesn't even seem as if the war is going on here, except for the fact that planes are always going overhead, north with their death loads.

Baby doll, I would plan to quit Lance around May 1 or May 15. I know I will be home sometime between those dates. Say, I'll take that back. I may not leave here until May 10. Gosh, I just don't know, Mary Alice. I tell you, why don't you plan to quit about two weeks after you get a cable from me in Japan. Also, why don't you see about how much an 8 mm movie projector will cost through Lance. I'm going to get one somehow. You may be able to make a good buy—they want you!

Mary Alice, I just keep living on the thought of how nice it will be to be around you and John. Gosh, it's going to take some real adjusting to get me used to it. I think that you are just the little girl that can make life beautiful. I'm just wondering if you can still handle things like you used to. Anyway, I'm looking forward to seeing you real soon.

Love you both very much,
Al

∞✕∞

Things had finally quieted down for Dad, and the end was clearly in sight. After all that he had gone through, he realized that it was going to take some real adjusting to get back to a normal civilian life.

After having read these letters so many times and discovering Dad's war experiences, I have a new perspective on what our veterans face on their return from service. We, as a nation, must support them in every way possible for the sacrifices they have made.

∞✕∞

20 APRIL 1952
SUNDAY

My darling Wife and John,

I now figure, for sure, that it is about 15 days before I go aboard ship at Inchon and head for Japan. You can look for a cable from me sometime around the sixth or seventh of May. It looks as if, to me, that I will not fly out, which I thought was a possibility. I don't know what ship I will be on, but I'll be there if everything goes OK.

Mary Alice, my mail has been rather fouled up since I've been here on Gimpo, so I'm not sure at all if I have received all my mail. Today, I got a card from you and John, Mother and Dad, and one letter from you. I've been so mail hungry that I've read them over and over several times. I do have duties here, but they are comparatively easy and you might say that I am on R & R. The weather here for the past few days has been very balmy, but every other day it changes to very rainy and cold. Needless to say, it is extremely better than the snow further north.

I sure thank you both for the Easter cards you sent. They were mighty cute. I'll bet John had a good time hunting Easter eggs the rabbit had left. I can hardly wait to see you two.

By the time you get this letter, it will only be a few days until you get a cable from me. The boat trip will be long, but I'll rest and get some of this Korean dirt out of my hide. As soon as I reach the States, I'll wire you when to expect me in. Right now, I plan to fly from the coast by military plane. Maybe you could meet me in Dallas or somewhere. Anyway, those details can be worked out later.

Baby, I expect I'll extend to stay in the Corps for a while longer. At least until school starts, or maybe even longer. How would you like to be stationed in Hawaii?

I had my teeth cleaned the other day and found, regardless of my neglect, they are still in good working order. Well, baby, it's been a long time, but now it's drawing to a close. So, here's hoping that I'll see you soon.

Your husband,
Al

P. S. I have sent a package home with some of my gear in it. It's coming by slow mail. Also, you should get some film from Dallas soon.

 ⚬⚬⚬

27 APRIL 1952

Dear Mary Alice and John,

Well, the news we have been waiting for has finally come! I am number one (1) on the list for rotation in May. I will leave Korea on or about the fifth of the month. Baby, as soon as I get to Japan, I'll wire you. You may get the wire before this letter arrives. I feel that I have done my share over here and I'm now ready to go home. This past week I have been moving around quite a lot. I joined the 1st Battalion 7th Marines for an air landing behind the main line. We went into position there in order to back the enemy, in case they try to come through. This was practice and is located across the river. After the drill was over, I came back here to Gimpo.

Sometime this next week, I will try and see Lagrone if I am down that way. I'm still teaching here in the regiment, and will continue to do so until around May 1, when I expect to be relieved. These people over here are exceptionally nice to me and my men. Fact about it, you might say we have found a home.

We don't know what to expect on May day?? Could be the Communist Chinese Forces (CCF) are planning a big celebration. I know we are planning one for them, even if they have forgotten it. I hope everything goes off quiet. It's getting too damn close now to mess up.

My mail is still fouled up and I know I haven't been getting all your mail. If I have missed some, it will catch up with me somewhere, sometime. I got two Easter cards from the church—I certainly did appreciate them.

Baby Doll, I want you to do some serious thinking about my staying in the Corps for a while. You see, I imagine I'll make captain before very long and the pay is mighty good. I doubt if I will ever have to go overseas again for some time now, and by that time we can get out. I believe we could get some money together as well and live fine for that time. Maybe we could save enough to get us a house started. Then I could go back to teaching school. I'll take my leave and then decide on what action we will take.

The days now seem long and drawn out, and it looks as if the fifth will never get here. However, I guess I'm just a little overanxious on my part. I'll be seeing you and our boy John in the very near future. I just want to hold both of you real close and love you and love you. You are about the cutest two people in all the world.

I love you so very much.

Your husband,
Al

5 MAY 1952

Dear Mary Alice and John,

Well, the day has come and I'm ready to leave anytime now. My gear is all packed, and all I'll have to do is pick it up and go. Along with this letter you will find two pictures, one of which is a very close study of me just before I leave the field.

Honey, you don't have to worry your little pretty head one bit about my coming home with my mustache, because I plan to shave it off once I get aboard ship. I understand it is not the style to wear them back in the States; however, mine here has been quite the thing. Here is how things are shaping up from here on in. Today, we will leave the 2nd Battalion and go from here to Munsan-ni and board a train that will take us to Inchon. From Inchon, we will go to Japan (Kobe). How long we will stay there, I do not know. It has been rumored around five days. I figure I should be in the states around three weeks from now. So, baby, this is the last letter you will get from me from here in Korea. I love you all very much and will see you soon.

Dad's handlebar mustache

Bye for now.
Al

❀

I am not sure exactly how Dad got back to the States from the war. Once he arrived in port, he probably took a plane to either Carswell Air Force Base in Ft. Worth or Love Field airport in Dallas. They were both an easy drive from Greenville, and I imagine that Mom and I (along with many family members) met him there. I'm sure it was a tearful reunion.

Chapter 17
COMMENDATION

Dad arrived back in Greenville around June 1, 1952, and he and Mom had a 30-day leave to decide what direction they would take. Dad had survived the war and realized it would take some time to re-adjust to a normal civilian lifestyle.

The women in the family were all excellent cooks and I'm sure Dad went from one meal to the next sampling typical east Texas fare like meatloaf, fried chicken, cornbread, black-eyed peas, vine-ripened tomatoes, and pecan pie. It was early summer, Greenville was in full bloom, the cicadas were starting to sing, and the bass were striking on the lakes. This was what Dad grew up with and loved. He had his wife and son and I'm sure it was a memorable month for the entire family.

On July 8, 1952, Dad received the following commendation from the Commanding General of the United States Marine Corps:

COMMENDATION

UNITED STATES MARINE CORPS
HEADQUARTERS
1ST MARINE DIVISION (REINF) FMF
SAN FRANCISCO, CALIFORNIA

The Commanding General, 1st Marine Division (Reinf) FMF, takes pleasure in commending

FIRST LIEUTENANT ALBERT G. HARRIS
UNITED STATES MARINE CORPS RESERVE

for service set forth in the following

CITATION:

"For excellent service in the line of his profession while serving with a Marine artillery battalion during operations against the enemy in KOREA from 12 February to 1 May 1952. First Lieutenant HARRIS, serving as an artillery liaison officer to an infantry battalion, displayed outstanding skill, courage and initiative in the performance of his duties. Working with a group of inexperienced forward observers he personally supervised their operations, thus ensuring that artillery fire was skillfully observed and adjusted. His tireless devotion to duty and sound technical knowledge resulted in excellent infantry-artillery relations, and was responsible for the effective coordination of fire delivered against the enemy. His actions were an inspiration to all who served with him and materially contributed to the success achieved by the battalion. First Lieutenant HARRIS' conduct throughout was in keeping with the highest traditions of the United States Naval Service."

Commendation Ribbon with Combat "V" Authorized.

J.T. SELDEN
Major General, U.S. Marine Corps
Commanding

On December 1, 1952, W. B. Partain, officer in charge of the Marine Corps Recruiting Station, Dallas, Texas, presented the Commendation Ribbon to Dad.

Presentation of Commendation Ribbon

Mom and Dad after the presentation

Chapter 18
POST-WAR HISTORY

Dad joined Magnolia Petroleum Corporation (now Mobil Oil Corporation) in late 1952. He spent most of his business career with Mobil and was transferred to various cities in Texas, Florida, and Colorado. In 1979, Dad moved back to Corpus Christi, Texas, and joined Everest Minerals Corporation as a land manager. He was a very successful businessman and in retirement continued as an independent investor in oil and gas projects.

Dad remained in the Marine Corps Reserve until 1960, when he was honorably discharged at the Naval Air Station in Corpus Christi with the rank of captain. In retirement, Dad loved going to the base and shopping at the PX, and he always received a snappy salute when he approached the guard house. Dad knew a colonel at the base and was invited to play golf on numerous occasions. (I was invited to ride along in the cart once.)

The aircraft carrier USS *Lexington* is dry-docked in Corpus Christi as a museum and tourist attraction. It was originally commissioned in 1943, the year Dad joined the Marines. In 1944, the *Lexington* joined the 5th fleet in Pearl Harbor and participated in nearly every major operation in the Pacific theater.

In the early 1960s, the *Lexington* was designated a Navy training carrier and in the mid 1960s, Dad had the opportunity to land on the *Lexington* during an actual training exercise. As a result, he received a certificate of admission to the "Tail Hook Club," which he proudly displayed in his office. You need to read *Devotion* by Adam Makos to get an appreciation of what it takes to land a plane on a World War II aircraft carrier!

Mom passed away on Christmas Day in 2006, at the age of 82. Dad had a Scottish bagpipe player lead the procession to her gravesite as a tribute to her Scottish heritage. Dad passed away on January 19, 2013, at the age of 87. He is buried next to Mom in Corpus Christi, and my sister and I arranged a military-style funeral. The honor guard from the Naval Air Station performed a twenty-one-gun salute, and it was truly a fitting tribute to our father, a decorated Korean War veteran.

And, yes, Dad did bring home the motion picture camera! On his return, he purchased a nice projector and screen and later some splicing/editing equipment. I do remember seeing movies taken in Korea, but my recollection is they were not of the war but of Dad and his buddies walking around smiling and waving, with tents and Korean hills in the background.

Dad made lots of movies. Every couple of months or so, he would get everything out, Mom would make popcorn, and we would watch home movies. This was a scene repeated throughout middle America in the 1950s and '60s. I miss many aspects of those simpler times.

Albert G. Harris

Mary Alice Harris

Toots Briton Banjo Band (Dad 3rd from right)

GLOSSARY

6 x 6 – six-wheel drive heavy duty truck
76 – 76 mm Russian artillery shell
82 – 82 mm Russian mortar shell
782 gear – field pack including canteen, poncho, ammo pouch, etc.

A-C

AWOL – absent without leave
BAR – Browning Automatic Rifle
BN – battalion
CAT – Caterpillar tractor
CCF – Communist Chinese Forces
CO – commanding officer
CP– Christmas party
C-ration – canned pre-cooked combat meal

D-G

DoD – Department of Defense
ETSTC – East Texas State Teachers College
FBI – Federal Bureau of Investigation
FDC – fire direction center
FMF – Fleet Marine Force
FO – forward observer
GE – General Electric
GI – government issue
GMC – General Motors Corporation
GPS – Global Positioning System

H-L

HP – horsepower
KIA – killed in action
KMC – Korean Marine Corps
KPA – Korean People's Army (North Korea)
KSC – Korean Supply Corporation
LCVP – Landing Craft, Vehicle, Personnel

M-N

MA – Mary Alice (Mom)
MARK – InterContinental Mark Hopkins Hotel
MC– Marine Corps
MPC – Military Payment Certificate
MSR – main supply route

MIA – missing in action
NATO – North Atlantic Treaty Organization
NBC – National Biscuit Corporation
NK – North Korean (soldier)
NKPA – North Korean People's Army
NROTC - Naval Reserve Officers Training Corps

P-T

PG – pregnant
POW – prisoner of war
PX – post exchange (military commissary)
R & R – rest and relaxation
ROK – Republic of Korea (South Korea)
RSOP – reconnaissance, selection, and occupation of position
S & W – Smith & Wesson
TOT – time on target

U-X

UN – United Nations
USO – United Service Organization
USS – United States Ship
WASP – Women Airforce Service Pilots
WIA – wounded in action
XO – executive officer (second in command)
XX – kisses

ACKNOWLEDGEMENTS

I would like to extend my sincere thanks to the following people for their help with *323 Days*:

To my Dad, Albert Harris, for taking the time to write these informative and loving letters on a regular basis during his tour of duty in the Korean War. He was committed to serving both his country and his family and was an inspiration to all of us growing up.

To my Mom, Mary Alice Harris, for saving Dad's letters over a sixty-two-year period as our family was transferred around the country with Mobil Oil Corporation. Wouldn't it be interesting if we also had Mom's letters, which inspired Dad to keep going during his difficult tour of duty? She too was an inspiration to us all.

To my wife, Joan Harris, who has helped me write, edit, and proofread business documents for the past forty-five years. She has taught me much about writing and editing, and her support and encouragement during this project have been extremely helpful. Her editing skills and attention to detail are first rate. Joan provided the final comprehensive edit of this book.

To my sister-in-law, Jan Whitacre, who was a senior technical writer for much of her business career. She helped proofread this book and made important suggestions regarding the format. Jan is my wife's identical twin.

To my sister, Amy Jones, who tirelessly took care of Mom and Dad during the last years of their lives. She did not have any substantive discussions with Dad about the war; however, she contributed significantly to this book with pictures, memories, and detailed proofreading. She also took Dad on many trips to the Corpus Christi Naval Air Station to shop at the PX, and she shared his enthusiasm for the Marine Corps and the many other activities he was involved in.

To my brother-in-law, Larry Jones, who knew Dad for more than thirty-three years. Larry is an avid gun enthusiast and had discussions with Dad regarding different firearms used during the war. Larry's recollections helped significantly in telling Dad's story.

To my sister's youngest son, Roger Jones, who is a graduate of Texas A & M University and the Dallas Theological Seminary. During high school, Roger interviewed Dad about the Korean War for a school project. His paper did not survive, but his recollections did. Roger was instrumental in helping piece together important events and facts not covered in Dad's letters.

And last, to Adam Makos for his outstanding books *Spearhead* and *Devotion*, which inspired me to transcribe and edit my father's firsthand account of the Korean War. Without either of Adam's books, this project most likely would not have happened. I look forward to reading his third book, *A Higher Call*, in the very near future.

REFERENCES

[1] "The Korean War (1950-1953) Summary", accessed August 8, 2019, https://www.sparknotes.com/history/american/koreanwar/summary/.

[2] "Korean War," last modified June 6, 2019, accessed August 8, 2019, https://www.history.com/topics/korea/korean-war.

[3] "Inchon Landing," History.com, last modified August 21, 2018, accessed May 4, 2019, https://www.history.com/topics/korea/inchon.

[4] "Interview: Melinda Pash, Why is Korea the 'Forgotten War'?", accessed August 8, 2019, https://www.historynet.com/interview-melinda-pash-why-is-korea-the-forgotten-war.htm.

[5] "Racial segregation in the United States Armed Forces," Wikipedia, accessed May 4, 2019, https://en.wikipedia.org/wiki/Racial_segregation_in_the_United_States_Armed_Forces.

[6] Adam Makos, *Devotion*, (New York: Ballantine Books, 2015), 200.

[7] Makos, *Devotion*, 200-201.

[8] "Marine Corps Jargon," accessed May 4, 2019, https://www.hqmc.marines.mil/Portals/143/Docs/Onboarding/Marine%20jargon.pdf.

[9] "LCVP (United States)," Wikipedia, accessed May 4, 2019, https://en.wikipedia.org/wiki/LCVP_(United_States).

[10] "Forward observers in the U.S. military," Wikipedia, accessed May 4, 2019, https://en.wikipedia.org/wiki/Forward_observers_in_the_U.S._military.

[11] "M1 carbine", Wikipedia, accessed August 2, 2019, https://en.wikipedia.org/wiki/M1_carbine.

[12] "List of ethnic slurs," Wikipedia, accessed May 4, 2019, https://en.wikipedia.org/wiki/List_of_ethnic_slurs.

[13] "Americans," The Racial Slur Database, accessed May 4, 2019, http://www.rsdb.org/race/americans.

[14] "M101 Howitzer," Wikipedia, accessed May 4, 2019, https://en.wikipedia.org/wiki/M101_Howitzer.

[15] "Cloyce Box," Wikipedia, accessed May 4, 2019, https://en.wikipedia.org/wiki/Cloyce_Box.

REFERENCES

[16] "Korean War and Self Inflicted Injuries," Lafayette College Special Collections, last modified November 15, 2012, https://sites.lafayette.edu/specialcollections/2012/11/15/korean-war-and-self-inflicted-injuries/.

[17] "Battle of the Punchbowl," Wikipedia, accessed May 4, 2019, https://en.wikipedia.org/wiki/Battle_of_the_Punchbowl.

[18] Matthew B. Ridgway, *The Korean War*, (New York: Doubleday, 1967), 187.

[19] "Vittori, Joseph," Korean War Medal of Honor Recipients, accessed May 4, 2019, https://history.army.mil/html/moh/koreanwar.html#VITTORI.

[20] John Nolan, *The Run-Up to the Punch Bowl*, (Xlibris Corporation, 2006), 163.

[21] "Whistling Death: How the Corsair Got Its Nickname," Fighter Sweep, accessed May 4, 2019, https://fightersweep.com/5378/whistling-death-corsair-nickname/.

[22] "M1918 Browning Automatic Rifle," Wikipedia, accessed August 2, 2019, https://en.wikipedia.org/wiki/M1918_Browning_Automatic_Rifle.

[23] "The Inside Story of the BAR, John M. Browning's Automatic Rifle," accessed August 2, 2019, https://www.browning.com/news/articles/the-inside-story-of-the-bar--john-m--browning-s-automatic-rifle.html.

[24] "Korean War Propaganda Leaflet Collection at the Library of Congress," Library of Congress, last modified September 26, 2017, https://blogs.loc.gov/international-collections/2017/09/korean-war-propaganda-leaflet-collection-at-the-library-of-congress/.

[25] "Women Airforce Service Pilots," Wikipedia, accessed July 9, 2019, https://en.wikipedia.org/wiki/Women_Airforce_Service_Pilots.

[26] "5 interesting facts about the Marines Corps birthday," We Are The Mighty, last modified November 9, 2016, https://www.wearethemighty.com/articles/5-interesting-facts-about-the-marine-corps-birthday.

[27] "Fire direction center definition (U.S. DoD)," accessed August 2, 2019, https://www.militaryfactory.com/dictionary/military-terms-defined.asp?term_id=2060.

[28] "Artillery: Time on Target," Wikipedia, accessed May 4, 2019, https://en.wikipedia.org/wiki/Artillery#Time_on_Target.

[29] Paul M. Edwards, *The Korean War, A Historical Dictionary,* (Maryland: Scarecrow Press, Inc., 2003), 184.

[30] "C-ration," Wikipedia, accessed May 4, 2019, https://en.wikipedia.org/wiki/C-ration.

[31] Makos, *Devotion,* 257.

PHOTO CREDITS

The following photos were licensed from Shutterstock.com:

- North/South Korea map

- Smith & Wesson .38 Special

- M1191 Colt .45

- M1 carbine

- 105 Howitzer graphic

- Squadron of Corsairs

- Landing at Inchon

The following photo was licensed from Bigstockphoto.com:

- M1918 Browning Automatic Rifle (BAR)

www.ingramcontent.com/pod-product-compliance
Lightning Source LLC
La Vergne TN
LVHW011224080426
835509LV00005B/295